Strategies for the Threshold #8

Dealing with Belial:
Spirit of Armies and Abuse

Anne Hamilton

Janice Speirs

Dealing with Belial: Spirit of Armies and Abuse

Strategies for the Threshold #8

© Anne Hamilton and Janice Speirs 2022

Published by Armour Books

P. O. Box 492, Corinda QLD 4075

Cover Images: © pierluigi1956 'Goats in high mountain pasture' | depositphotos.com; lighthouse '3d illustration of an Angel in grass field' | depositphotos.com; iloveotto 'Asia style textures and backgrounds' | canstockphoto.com

Section Divider Images: © cundrawan703 | canstockphoto.com

Interior Design and Typeset by Beckon Creative

ISBN: 978-1-925380-48-4

 A catalogue record for this book is available from the National Library of Australia

All rights reserved. No part of this publication may be reproduced, stored in, or introduced into a retrieval system, or transmitted, in any form, or by any means (electronic, mechanical, photocopying, recording or otherwise) without the prior written permission of the publisher.

Note: Australian spelling and grammar conventions are used throughout this book.

Strategies for the Threshold #8

Dealing with Belial:
Spirit of Armies and Abuse

Anne Hamilton

Janice Speirs

Unless otherwise noted, Scripture quotations are taken from the Holy Bible, New International Version®, NIV®. Copyright © 1973, 1978, 1984, 2011 by Biblica, Inc.™ Used by permission of Zondervan. All rights reserved worldwide. www.zondervan.com The "NIV" and "New International Version" are trademarks registered in the United States Patent and Trademark Office by Biblica, Inc.™.

Scripture quotations marked AMP are taken from the Amplified Version of the Bible Copyright © 2015 by The Lockman Foundation, La Habra, CA 90631. All rights reserved. www.lockman.org

Scripture quotations marked BLB are taken from The Blue Letter Bible. Used by permission. blueletterbible.org

Scripture quotations marked BSB are taken from The Holy Bible, Berean Study Bible, BSB Copyright ©2016 by Bible Hub Used by Permission. All Rights Reserved Worldwide.

Scripture quotations marked CEV are from the Contemporary English Version Copyright © 1991, 1992, 1995 by American Bible Society. Used by Permission.

Scripture quotations marked ESV are taken from the ESV® Bible (The Holy Bible, English Standard Version®), copyright © 2001 by Crossway, a publishing ministry of Good News Publishers. Used by permission. All rights reserved.

Scripture quotations marked ISV are taken from the Holy Bible: International Standard Version®. Copyright © 1996-forever by The ISV Foundation. ALL RIGHTS RESERVED INTERNATIONALLY. Used by permission.

Scripture quotations marked KJV are taken from the King James Version of the Bible. Public domain.

Scripture quotations marked NASB are taken from the New American Standard Bible®, Copyright © 1960, 1962, 1963, 1968, 1971, 1972, 1973, 1975, 1977, 1995 by The Lockman Foundation. Used by permission. (www.Lockman.org)

Scripture quotations marked NLT are taken from the Holy Bible, New Living Translation, copyright 1996, 2004. Used by permission of Tyndale House Publishers, Inc., Wheaton, Illinois 60189. All rights reserved.

Scripture quotations marked NIV are taken from the Holy Bible, New International Version®, NIV®. Copyright © 1973, 1978, 1984, 2011 by Biblica, Inc.™ Used by permission of Zondervan. All rights reserved worldwide. www.zondervan.com The "NIV" and "New International Version" are trademarks registered in the United States Patent and Trademark Office by Biblica, Inc.™.

Scripture quotations marked NKJV are taken from the New King James Version. Copyright © 1982 by Thomas Nelson, Inc. Used by permission. All rights reserved.

Scripture quotations marked NRS are taken from New Revised Standard Version of the Bible, copyright 1952 [2nd edition, 1971] by the Division of Christian Education of the National Council of the Churches of Christ in the United States of America. Used by permission. All rights reserved.

Scripture quotations marked TPT are taken from The Passion Translation®, *Luke and Acts: To the Lovers of God* copyright © 2014 by Broadstreet Publishing. Used by permission. All rights reserved. ThePassionTranslation.com

Scripture quotations marked WEB are taken from the World English Bible, a modernisation of the American Standard Version (ASV). Public domain.

Other Books By Anne Hamilton

In this series

Dealing with Python: Spirit of Constriction
(with *Arpana Dev Sangamithra*)

Dealing with Ziz: Spirit of Forgetting

Name Covenant: Invitation to Friendship

Hidden in the Cleft: True and False Refuge

Dealing with Leviathan: Spirit of Retaliation

Dealing with Resheph: Spirit of Trouble
(with *Irenie Senior*)

Dealing with Azazel: Spirit of Rejection

Devotional Theology series

God's Poetry: The Identity & Destiny Encoded in Your Name

God's Panoply: The Armour of God & the Kiss of Heaven

God's Pageantry: The Threshold Guardians
& the Covenant Defender

God's Pottery: The Sea of Names & the Pierced Inheritance

God's Priority: World-Mending & Generational Testing

More Precious than Pearls (with *Natalie Tensen*)

As Resplendent As Rubies (with *Natalie Tensen*)

As Exceptional as Sapphires (with *Donna Ho*)

Spiritual Legal Rights (with *Janice Sergison*)

Jesus and the Healing of History Series

\# 1 ***Like Wildflowers, Suddenly***
\# 2 ***Bent World, Bright Wings***
\# 3 ***Silk Shadows, Rings of Gold***
\# 4 ***Where His Feet Pass***
\# 5 ***The Singing Silence***

Contents

Acknowledgments		9
Introduction		13
1	**Coffee and Covenant**	19
	Prayer	29
2	**Time, and Time Again**	33
	Prayer	66
3	**Stealing Healing**	69
	Prayer	109
4	**Tests and Tabernacles**	113
	Prayer	137
5	**The Cornerstone and the Cloud**	139
	Preparation and Prayer	163
6	**'We have met the enemy...'**	167
	Prayer	188
7	**Replacing the Cornerstone**	191
	Prayer	216
Appendix 1	Summary	219
Appendix 2	Summary of Belial's Main Tactics	227
Appendix 3	Types of Complicity	229
Appendix 4	'Dat Ribber in Egypt'	243
Appendix 5	Belial and the Number 153	245
Endnotes		251

Acknowledgments

I'M WRITING THIS ON THE DAY after my mother's funeral. An ending as well as a new beginning for our family. A threshold moment.

In each generation, God calls individuals to 'mend the world' by repairing specific wounds that their ancestors have inflicted or received. He also has a high calling for the family as a whole, one which—if not completed in one generation—is passed on to the next. Usually becoming more tangled, complex and toxic in the process.

My mother suffered various kinds of abuse as a child. She didn't talk about it, except on rare occasions when it was helpful for others to realise she shared in the kinds of suffering they were going through—and that it is possible to overcome even the most difficult circumstances. If there was any book in this series where I was looking forward to her input, it was this one above all. She had a 'nose' for abuse; or maybe it was simply that experience led her to give less of the benefit of the doubt to people when even the tiniest of red-flag behaviours were on display.

I particularly miss my mum's wisdom when it came to crafting prayers. She always worried that hers weren't 'good enough' and I would always have to say: 'Mum, it's not about you. It's doesn't matter if it's inadequate. Mine would be no less inadequate. It doesn't have to be perfect, it just has to connect people with the hem of Jesus' prayer shawl so He can make them perfect.' So although I feel inadequate to fill in for my mother, I remind myself of my own words to her: it's not about flawless wording but only about the link the words create with Yeshua HaMaschiah, Jesus our Messiah.

A huge **thank you** to those who've given so freely of their time, insights and inspiration to make this book better than it would have otherwise been: Janice Speirs, Anne Porter, Sean Quental, Rebekah Robinson, Donna Ho, Quang Hii, Josefine Lim, Mary Warren, Joy and Richard Senior, Susan Brunt, Alex McLaughlin, Cathy McCarter Olsen, Julie Kempt and Arpana Dev Sangamithra.

As usual, this book is written in numerical literary style. Its sections are designed with number patterning, in a similar way to the scenes of Scripture. This book is also written in a non-linear style—I term the way it's constructed as 'kaleidoscopic'. Greek thinking is linear, Hebrew thinking is block, and 'kaleidoscopic' is somewhere in the middle. It's a transitional form. I realise how culturally we are embedded in rationalist linear thinking; however, until we start to teach our brains to think in a more Hebraic way, we'll always be constrained by the limitations of logic—a field that simply does not handle paradox well. Scripture is rich and replete with paradox, along with superficial contradictions that usually need serious digging in order to resolve.

So—may Love bring you under the shadow of His wing and show you His glory.

Anne Hamilton
Brisbane, Australia 2022

Introduction

Several years ago, I realised I was going to have to write a book on the spirit of abuse. It's one of the threshold guardians, after all. It's one of those fallen angelic majesties that come to test us as we approach the doorway into our calling. So, since this series focuses on how to deal with such spirits, it was a given that, sooner or later, I'd have to get around to it. I consequently decided I was going to have to research far more than usual because, well, I've never experienced very much abuse in my life.

God must have laughed when I told Him that. And He must have laughed even more heartily when I said that I'd stood against abuse but I had very little acquaintance about the spirit behind it. That was three and a half years ago when I was seeking His guidance on where to direct my attention. Since that time, I've intensively researched abuse through many books, thousands of articles, dozens of stories of people known to me personally. I was particularly interested in learning to discern the methodology of the spirit behind all the abuse. It's one thing to be able to recognise abuse, quite another to see how all the disparate cords woven together by this spirit enable it to operate so effectively on a vast, worldwide, cross-cultural scale.

Abuse is such a broad topic that I initially chose a very selective focus: how this spirit operates in church settings once it has been exposed. My particular interest was in investigating how authorities—both individuals and hierarchies—respond to allegations of abuse. How do believers, singly or in groups, deal with the spirit behind it all? It quickly became apparent that the answer was: *very badly.*

Just as I had drafted a couple of chapters, I got a serious foot infection and had to keep my leg elevated for some months. During that time, when I couldn't use a computer, I read a lot. I also said to the Lord, 'Why isn't this foot healing? What's this about?'

'You don't understand abuse,' He said. 'Take a step back.'

I didn't think my foot infection could have anything to do with what I was writing but, mentally, I took a step back and tried to get a wide-angle view of abuse. I researched the symbolism of 'foot' and 'step' in Scripture and realised there was indeed a strong link to the spirit of abuse. And I also started to see the spirit behind abuse had an entirely different and unexpected face. It even had several names, other than the ones I'd already discerned.

With this new knowledge, I thought I was ready to begin again on the book, but God said, 'Take another step back.'

My mother would have been impressed. She always said that, when God spoke to her, He did so in four-word sentences. And while He usually talks to me in weird and wonderful, completely perplexing symbols, throughout this time it was all four-word sentences.

In the 1970s, during a bank robbery gone wrong in the Swedish capital, Stockholm, a thief took four hostages and held them in a vault for six days. During this time, a rapport was established between the robber and his captives to such a degree that, after their release, the hostages not only refused to testify against their captor but actually raised money for his legal defence.

Subsequently, whenever hostages develop positive psychological bonds with their captors, their condition is often referred to as 'Stockholm Syndrome'. A similar situation can sometimes occur with abuse victims who develop an attachment to the perpetrator, and so resist healing as a result. Until God told me to 'take a step back', I didn't realise that such a relationship can develop not only between abused and abuser, but between abused and the spirit of abuse.

I woke up suddenly to my own complicity with the spirit of abuse. I was collaborating with the enemy. And, as I described my behaviour to other people, I realised how prevalent this condition was. Like me, they were shocked to suddenly recognise they'd been taken hostage and they'd slid ever so slowly into the unthinkable: siding with the enemy of God—and not even realising it!

So, once again, the focus of this book changed. It's now completely different in purpose. It's no longer really about abuse, or even about the spirit of abuse, but it's about how we unknowingly become complicit with this spiritual hostage-taker, and what needs to happen *before* we can even begin to tackle this spirit successfully.

Belial is different. With Python, Ziz or Leviathan, the right Fruit of the Spirit make an incredible difference. With Azazel, there's a helpful procedure to follow to be able to claim the particular Fruit of the Spirit needed in that instance—but ultimately, that procedure is simply a variation on repenting of a false refuge. However, with Belial, it was easy to see that more, much more, than elimination of false refuges and claiming of Fruit and kissing on God's armour was needed. Jesus—*of course!*—was the answer, but in a very special way.

When I wrote *God's Pottery: The Sea of Names and the Pierced Inheritance*, I talked about the need for a replacement cornerstone with a new inscription. Part of the procedure for passing over the threshold into your calling involves a new foundation stone. At the time, I didn't know why it was necessary to acquire a replacement, just that the Holy Spirit said it was so. Now—six years later—I understand the reasons. I also realise I missed something. Something essential, at least when it comes to Belial. More than likely, this book misses something too. But like my other books, it's a starting point for a dialogue, not the last word on the subject.

Before reading this book, I recommend you work through *Hidden in the Cleft: True and False Refuge.*

If you want to go further after reading this book, I recommend *God's Pottery: The Sea of Names and the Pierced Inheritance*, which has, in its last chapter, a series of fourteen steps to progress through as guidelines for tackling the 'threefold guard' that forms the main obstacle to getting across the threshold into our calling. Sample prayers for each step are in the appendices to *God's Pottery.*

If you realise that you were looking for a book on abuse, rather than the spirit of abuse, check out Mary deMuth's *We Too: How the Church Can Respond Redemptively to the Sexual Abuse Crisis.*

May God's healing flow to you as you read on.

1
Coffee and Covenant

COFFEE.

Sitting and brooding over a cup of coffee.

In an earlier book in this series, *Hidden in the Cleft*, I described the long years of disappointment regarding my life's calling. Over the decades, my hope had been repeatedly crushed because God seemed absent during times of critical opportunity. But one day He revealed that, when I was troubled, I calmed my spirit with a cup of coffee, instead of seeking Him first. I'd had no idea that the real issue was finding comfort in the 'good' rather than in God. And I was able to overlook my behaviour by trotting out various theological excuses for why things went wrong. I'd never actually asked God why events hadn't turned out as I'd hoped and prayed and fervently believed for.

Now I'm not going to retell all that backstory here. But I do want to highlight what happened *after* I expressed my sorrow to God for substituting coffee as my refuge—instead of Him.

Shortly after repenting, I found myself disappointed again. I received yet another rejection of a manuscript I'd sent off to a publisher. This time, however, instead of heading for the coffee, I went straight to God. And as I asked Him what went wrong, He impressed on me how ambiguous the wording in the rejection letter was. As I sensed He was telling me the reviewers intended to steal the central core of my idea, I sighed, 'This always happens to me whenever I put even a toenail over the line into an area for which I'm not qualified.'

As soon as I spoke, I realised its significance. *This always happens to me...* It was a statement containing the word, *'always'.* From my training in prayer ministry, I knew I'd expressed a vow. I thought long and hard about the statement, turning it over in my mind. I reworked and reshaped it, looking for the wording that sat just right within my spirit. At last I was able to identify the vow: *I will always be robbed whenever I step into an area where I'm not qualified.*

That seemed inordinately strange. Generally, vows are the result of traumatic childhood experiences. Yet I couldn't imagine any child saying: 'I will always be robbed whenever I step into an area where I'm not qualified.' Children don't think that way; they aren't qualified for anything!

Besides, qualifications shouldn't have any impact whatsoever on any spiritual calling! I knew the old saying: *God doesn't call the qualified, He qualifies the called.* And I truly believed it.

There's an extremely good reason for God operating this way: if we were qualified to do the job He has for us, we'd rely on our *own* strength, not *His*. Any calling He has for us is so far beyond us that it's utterly essential to rely on Him. If our first instinctive response when He presents our calling to us isn't 'No! I can't do that! That's way beyond me!' then it's probably not our calling.

Nevertheless, I realised the vow was a hindrance. If being unqualified was—ironically—the first qualification for a divine calling, then a vow about being robbed due to lack of qualifications was going to be an Everest of a problem. But where had the vow originated? If it wasn't from childhood, then it had to come from one of my parents or grandparents. That same hour I went to see my mother to ask her if anything like this had ever happened to her. She shook her head.

'What about dad?' I asked.

My dad had died several months previously so I couldn't ask him directly. However, it seemed highly unlikely. In fact, just the opposite. My dad had reached the top of his profession despite lacking formal qualifications. He'd mentioned once that he'd been quietly advised never to reveal he hadn't been to university because he'd just been promoted above several candidates who had. In fact, my dad had been such a quiet achiever that, at his funeral, my mother was approached by an engineering professor who remarked that our family seemed unaware of my father's worldwide reputation for excellence and efficiency in the generation of electricity. Engineers from around the globe visited him on inspection tours.

All this suggested any issue about qualifications definitely was not coming from my dad but, still, it was worth checking.

'He never mentioned anything,' my mum said.

'What about his mother or father? Or your mother and father?' I asked.

My mother didn't know of anything. It was an impasse. God had answered me but, within an hour, I was back to the stumbling block once more.

The following day I drove my niece to a prayer ministry course. She'd recently got her driving licence but she wasn't confident negotiating traffic all the way to the far side of town. I'd volunteered to drive her and, because going back and forward twice would take so much out of the day, I decided to enroll in the course as a repeat student.

When the time came for the small group session, the leader decided I was going to be the one to receive ministry. I protested. I pointed out there were others who should be given precedence. However the leader wouldn't hear of it. So I racked my brains for a spiritual problem that was weighing on my heart as unresolved.

This matter of qualifications...

I explained to the group my belief that God had called me to be a writer and my weird vow about qualifications that seemed to have no basis in my own life or that of my ancestors.

The leader frowned and, opening her Bible, she began flipping through the pages. I thought she was about to read an encouraging Scripture but instead she pulled out a strip of paper. She read it aloud: *whenever I was about to receive a reward for my hard work, someone with more qualifications would cut in and push me out, taking the promotion I'd earned.*

'Yes!' I exclaimed. 'That describes the situation almost exactly. Where did that come from?'

'Those are your father's words,' the leader said.

I stared at her in disbelief. *What were my father's words doing in her Bible?*

'I went to visit him just a couple of months before he died,' she said. 'And when he said that, I thought, "You'll want to deal with the issues behind that when you recover," so I wrote them down to make sure I could speak to him later about what he'd said. They've been sitting in my Bible ever since.'

To say I was stunned is to vastly underrate my feelings. Not even my mother knew that my dad believed this! I wondered if he had ever realised he had a worldwide reputation for excellence and efficiency in electrical power generation. If he had, he'd never seen fit to mention it. In fact, although my mother had helped him entertain many international visitors on occasion, she was quite sure they'd been on a junket. I rather suspected she'd absorbed my father's view, and that his vow about qualifications blinded him.

This revelation was so unexpected. I thought about the myriad tiny choices—volunteering to bring my niece to the course, deciding to repeat rather than go back and forth in traffic, being selected for just this group, the leader's insistence I *had* to be the one to receive ministry, the fact that on any other day I probably would not have mentioned anything about qualifications, the fact my dad had said something to this woman he hadn't ever told anyone else and she had felt it significant enough to write down—and the fact that, almost a year later, that slip of paper was still in her Bible.

It was self-evidently God's perfect timing. I immediately set about renouncing this generational vow. As I did, I heard the Holy Spirit speak. 'While you're at it,' He said, 'you might also renounce your covenant with Death.'

I had no idea what that meant. 'The Holy Spirit is talking about the covenant with Death,' I said to the leader, hoping she could explain. But she had no idea either.

'Okay then,' I went on, 'I have no idea what a covenant with Death actually is, but I'm just going to follow this prompt.' So out loud, in front of witnesses, I renounced a covenant with Death.

And everything changed. Not immediately, not for several months—but so suddenly and spectacularly when the breakthrough came, there was no mistaking it.

In the meantime, I'd unearthed a pair of Scripture verses that referenced a covenant with Death. And there, sandwiched between them, was a completely baffling prophecy about a cornerstone laid in Zion. What I didn't realise until very recently was that it was about replacing one already there.

> *Thus says the Lord God, 'Behold, I am the One Who has laid as a foundation in Zion, a stone, a tested stone, a precious cornerstone, of a sure foundation: "Whoever believes will not be in haste."'*
>
> Isaiah 28:16 ESV

The inscribed cornerstone in Zion is the climax of Isaiah 28. On the surface, that chapter of Isaiah's prophecy is a chaotic jumble of images that ebb and flow like flotsam on a storm-wracked shore. It takes a long wade into its deeper waters before it becomes apparent that there's a single unity of thought behind it. It takes even longer to realise that it outlines God's blueprint for dealing with abuse—in all its facets.

The chapter starts out with a warning to some drunkards in Samaria, then exalts God as the true head of Israel, shifts focus to encouraging watchmen who will turn back the battle at the gates, follows on with some remarks about babbling babies, throws in the most frequently misused and decontextualised verse in all Scripture, takes a swipe at people who rely on false refuges and covenants with Death, prophesies about a divinely ordained and engraved cornerstone, circles back to explain that God will void our covenants with Death, mutters on about the width and length of beds and blankets, recaptures that fleeting thought about covenants with Death and tells us that God will sign off on His annulment of them through unnatural weather phenomena or astronomical aberrations, all before finishing up with a discussion of different seeds and a variety of farming and threshing techniques.

Back and forward it goes in what seems like a mess of random, disconnected thoughts. It darts and weaves, and makes you wonder what Isaiah had been imbibing that day.

In fact, Isaiah 28 is an exquisitely constructed poem. In the Hebrew style, it is created in a mirror-reflective pattern around a central summit: and that's the verse describing the inscribed cornerstone that God will lay in Zion.

Now of course, in the fullness of time, it transpired that this Cornerstone was Jesus. He said so Himself and so did both Peter and Paul in their epistles. In fact, when I first came to examine this verse as I tried to unravel what it had to do with a covenant with Death, all I could find by way of insight in various commentaries was a lot of circular reasoning that went like this: the cornerstone in Isaiah refers to Jesus because Peter and Paul say so, and they say so because Isaiah prophesied it was so.

Except, of course, Isaiah doesn't mention Jesus by name. Frankly, I was curious to know why Paul and Peter were both inspired to choose this particularly subtle quote when there are much more obvious ones on offer. Their attitudes seem to be: 'Aha! See! Isn't this just the best? Wow! All about Jesus. Self-evident.'

But it wasn't self-evident to me. What was there they could see that I couldn't? Well, after I'd been disappointed by several commentaries, I simply asked God.

It took a couple of months before He answered and, when He did, it was in a strange symbol. Hinges started acting up. The front door, a door at work, cupboards at home, one at church, even my knee—suddenly, over a matter of just few days, all sorts of hinges misbehaved. Now one or two would have been a nuisance and an inconvenience, but this looked like a pattern. On the off-chance it was 'dark speech' from God, I looked up *hinge* in Scripture.

And there, eventually, in a commentary on Isaiah 57:8–9 about doors, doorposts, door cavities and hinges, I read for the first time about a *threshold covenant* and its relationship to the cornerstone laid in Zion. I'd never heard of a threshold covenant before and no one I spoke to had either. I thanked God for answering my prayer and set out to uncover what this unknown covenant was. The first book I came across specifically devoted to the topic was Henry Clay Trumbull's *The Threshold Covenant*.[1] It explained just enough to get me started. I never imagined I would write an entire series on the different aspects of threshold covenants. Or how an understanding of it would open up so many mysterious episodes in Scripture.

This book in your hands at the moment focuses not so much on the spirit of abuse as on the preparation you need to undertake before you can even think about overcoming it. You need to be equipped with more than the Armour of God, you need more than proficiency in the appropriate use of the Fruit of the Spirit. You need the right divine covering of two kinds: Cornerstone and Cloud. Every Scriptural story about the spirit of abuse that ends in triumph—and there aren't many—has those special elements: the Cornerstone and the Cloud.

Prayer

The following prayer is almost identical to the one in *Hidden in the Cleft*, the fourth book in this series. That book is about false refuges. When people ask me for help with threshold issues, particularly with the throne guardians who watch over them, my answer is always that the first step is to identify and repent of your false refuges. So even though there are many clues in this book about overcoming the spirit of abuse, they can only remain in the realm of the theoretical until you have dealt with your false refuges.

The prayer from *Hidden in the Cleft* repenting of false refuges is reproduced here because, even if you've read that book and prayed the prayer, it's likely that the Lord has revealed one or two or even a handful of false refuges since you did. He's always revealing hidden ones to me! In fact, you'll read about one in the next chapter.

As always in the books in this series, the prayers provided are not meant as a formula but as a starting point. Sometimes, at the end of a chapter, you may realise you've got exactly the problem outlined—but you don't know where to begin to talk to God about it. That's why the prayers are there—to help overcome those initial blockages. Please use them that way, not as an end in themselves.

Father God, I hold on to the tassels of Love's cloak—the prayer shawl of Jesus, my mediator—and I ask Him to intercede for me before Your throne. You know I can't do this, but He can. You know that half of me desperately wants to repent and to be the one to take an axe to my false refuges—my habits of consolation and my coping mechanisms—and smash them beyond repair. You also know that the other half of me wants to fortify them and decorate them with even more creature comforts.

So, Father, although I am about to say, 'I repent', it's only true if Jesus comes to empower my words through His cross, His blood and His wounds.

Father, I repent of grieving you through my unbelief and wounding Your heart.

Father, I repent of using fleshly consolations and ways of coping out of my unbelief in the atonement.

Father, I repent of ever treating your gifts of repentance, forgiveness and reconciliation at the cross of Jesus as a formula.

Father, I repent of my patchwork of belief and unbelief which leads to mockery of the atonement.

Father, I repent of allowing those stony parts of my heart to continue to refuse to accept the all-sufficiency of the sacrifice of Jesus.

Father, I acknowledge that these words I have just spoken do nothing unless the atonement of Jesus empowers them.

Father, I now ask You to direct Your angel axemen to descend and to chop down these false refuges so that they can never be rebuilt.

Father, I give You permission to command that every stronghold of my life that dishonours You is smashed so that not one stone is left upon another.

Father, I ask You to rewire my neural processes and the networks in my brain so that I can take these thoughts and habits captive and present them to You.

Father, I ask for Your love to overshadow me and Your grace to empower me as Your Spirit leads me into an ever-stronger belief in the all-sufficiency of Jesus' sacrifice for me.

Father, I will need the help of Jesus, my mediator, and of the Holy Spirit, my advocate, as I face the test that lies before me. Please send them speedily to my aid when the time comes. Please alert me as I enter the test and remind me to seek You first, foremost and always.

I thank You and bless You for making this redemption possible. I praise the name of Jesus of Nazareth. I confess Him as Lord of my life. And just as Your chosen people still tuck prayers into the crevices of the western wall in the City where You have placed Your name, so I ask Jesus to tuck me into the wound in His side and hide me from all the power of the enemy.

I declare You to be my true refuge, now and always. And I ask the Holy Spirit to prompt me to keep under cover whenever I am tempted to come out from the shelter of Your covenant.

Thank You, Father, for Your kiss that clothes me in Your armour. May Your name be praised throughout all ages.

Blessing and honour and glory and power belong to You and to the Lamb forever and ever. Amen.

2

Time, and Time Again

I'D SIGNED UP FOR A WORKSHOP at a local school and, when I arrived, discovered it was being held in a breezy, open courtyard, shaded by high sun-sails. The school chaplain greeted those attending with a curious admission: she felt a sense of unease, she said, to welcome us all to a spot that had once been an aboriginal bora ring—a place of power where initiation ceremonies had been conducted in times past.

If you are spiritually sensitive, you will probably relate to her sense of unease. Just how do we tread respectfully in the sacred spaces of cultures other than our own, particularly ones with which we disagree? Scripture, after all, tells us not to hold anyone in contempt—*anyone at all*. It goes so far as to include unholy powers and fallen angels in the category of *'anyone'*. Jude and Peter both inform us of the dire consequences of ignoring this warning. We are not to ridicule, revile, deride or disrespect even the satan himself.

I've encountered some very eerie places over the years. I've felt dread looking into a circle of carvings high on a mountainside, I've sensed something sinister lurking in the vicinity of a ring of stones on a heath, I often have to forestall the rising sense of panic I feel whenever I even see an invitation to walk a labyrinth. Some places simply exude wild fear and an unearthly aura of raw power.

Our natural inclination is to avoid such disturbing settings. Yet our ancestors tended to build churches and chapels slap bang on top of such places—a practice all too often denounced today as, at best, ignorant and foolish and, at worst, complicit with idolatry. Many believers in our era are adamant that, by establishing Christian communities over pagan sacred sites, past generations not only brought down heavy defilement on themselves, but also passed that corruption on down to us.

It's a pity that we can't transport this disquiet we rightly feel about these numinous landscapes into the pages of Scripture. Because it's all too easy to be blind to its record. When it comes to spiritual warfare, building redemptively on tainted sites is actually one of God's battle strategies. He did it regarding the Temple in Jerusalem, with its foundation on a Jebusite threshing floor—and thus almost certainly a pagan portal for divination and spirit contact.[2]

Jesus too adopts the very same kind of tactic. He didn't shy away from the menace surrounding unholy places. Instead He deliberately provoked the powers of darkness. He entered 'their' territory, took His stand and declared war. It's easy to miss that proclamation because so much else happened at the same moment. He was in fact creating the cornerstone for His church in one of the most famous—as well as the most despoiled—places in the entire ancient world: the so-called 'Gates of Hell' at a pagan shrine in Caesarea Philippi.

What is a *cornerstone?*

The word is a favourite in Christian circles, but it's rarely, if ever, explained. At least that's my experience.

What image springs to mind for you when the word *'cornerstone'* is mentioned? For some people it's four sandstone-like blocks, positioned at the corners of an imposing old house or office tower. For others, it's a foundation stone—a brass plaque or marble slab inscribed with the date—naming various dignitaries associated with an official opening. For still others, it's simply the brick that unites two intersecting walls.

The ancient meaning is quite different. Originally, it referred to the very first stone laid down in the construction of a dwelling. This stone marked the doorway—then commonly positioned at the corner of the house, hence *cornerstone*. There was only one cornerstone, not four. Unlike the stones of the walls or floor, it had a shallow basin carved into its upper surface. This bowl was designed to catch blood that dripped down from the lintels and doorposts whenever an animal was slaughtered during Passover rites, or a guest was welcomed for a feast.

The cornerstone was, in essence, a sacrificial altar. It was sacred, holy, consecrated, set apart, perhaps with an engraved inscription. You didn't touch it, you would *pass over* it. If you did touch it, even by stumbling, you would profane it—you were, in fact, seen to be refusing a covenant offered by the host. Accident was one thing but, if you were intentional about rejecting the covenant offered, you'd deliberately strike the stone or dash your foot against it.

A cornerstone was where threshold covenant was solemnised. And it wasn't just houses that had cornerstones. Tents and temples did. So did towns and cities. Nations had them. The universe itself has one. God told Job so:

> *Where were you when I laid the foundations of the earth?*
> *Tell Me, if you have understanding.*
> *Who fixed its measurements? Surely you know!*
> *Or who stretched a measuring line across it?*
> *On what were its foundations set,*
> *or who laid its **cornerstone**,*
> *while the morning stars sang together*
> *and all the sons of God shouted for joy?*
>
> Job 38:4–7 BSB

The cornerstone Jesus gave His church was fashioned from a response of faith, a confession of identity, a revelation not of flesh-and-blood but of the Holy Spirit. The Word of God took a few simple words and set them in place as a cornerstone:

> *'You are Peter, and on this rock I will build My church, and the gates of Hades will not overcome it.'*
>
> Matthew 16:18 NIV

These words correspond to the moment of conception for the 'living stones' of His *ekklesia*—they began the birth process that would culminate nearly nine months later at Pentecost.

Now this may come as a surprise, but people also have cornerstones. You and I have one. And, in the natural order of things, they're invariably and irreparably damaged.

My dad might have had a worldwide reputation for excellence and efficiency in his profession but he was the poster boy for workaholism. Very late in his life the possibility was raised that, in a different era, he might have been diagnosed with Asperger's Syndrome—very high functioning, admittedly, but still on the spectrum. His condition meant he was ideal for a job in which safety was top priority: things had to be *perfect* before he would sign off on them.

Great in the electricity industry; not so wondrous in human relationships. My parents' marriage struggled. Then one day, everything changed. The switching in his mind was rerouted and, in the darkness, a series of lights flickered on. Nothing was ever the same. My dad had gone with my sister and brother-in-law to hear John Sandford speak while my mother minded the grandchildren. He was to swap places with her the following day so she could attend the second half of the seminar. But that evening, he made a momentous announcement: 'You know, the problems in our marriage might *not* be all your fault, after all.'

After my mum picked her jaw up off the floor, she insisted my dad return to the seminar the following day. She was more than happy to keep baby-sitting if there was any chance someone could convince my father he had his own share of unresolved issues.

So began my parents' involvement with Elijah House Ministries. Their lives underwent radical transformation. What impacted my father the most was a teaching on pre-natal woundings. 'I tick every single box when it comes to symptoms for children conceived out of wedlock,' he said. 'But that doesn't make any sense at all. My parents were married.'

But his symptoms were so strong—particularly the sense of being unwanted and rejected—he felt it had to be investigated. Both his parents had passed away but he had a pair of maiden aunts he could ask. They immediately confirmed the truth of what he suspected.

'It was the deepest secret,' they told him. 'You were said to be sickly and premature and were fed via an eyedropper for the first month. But no one was much fooled. Your grandparents treated your parents viciously. And the worst of all was our discovery after your grandparents died. We found their wedding certificate: and it turned out they'd always lied about the year they married. They spent their lives hiding the fact your grandmother was pregnant with your mother at the ceremony, so treating her the way they did later was unbelievably hypocritical.'

Behind my dad's workaholism and drive for perfection was the insatiable need: *approve of me, don't reject me, want me, want me, want me, accept me, accept me, accept me, love me, love me, love me.*

He came a long, long way in the last years of his life—but, as my mother often said, it was a core wounding and it never did get fully healed. He'd receive prayer for rejection and it would clear up for a few months, but then it would return—as bad as ever.

Why won't this heal permanently? That's what I would always wonder. Jesus, after all, came to heal the broken-hearted and that's exactly what *broken-hearted* means: a core wounding. *So why does the issue keep returning?* My mother was always convinced it was a spirit of rejection that was cast out but kept returning—and she was right.

But I kept wondering: *what legal right would a spirit of rejection have to keep on returning time after time?*

Eventually I realised—long after my dad passed away—that it's not so much about casting out this spirit as *overcoming* it. That's the message of Scripture to us. We must *master* it.

This spirit is attached to the cornerstone of our personal being. Or, if the spirit of rejection isn't crouched there, another of the threshold guardians is.

In one sense, we all have core woundings. Some of us are more horrifically mutilated than others, but all of us suffer from damage to our inmost self. Our cornerstone—the very foundation of our identity and destiny—is cracked, and we have no power within ourselves to fix it.

If the very beginning of our beginning is impaired, how can we ourselves ever rectify our own being? If we've been built crookedly right from the start, how can our defects possibly be overcome?

Scripture spells out the answer very clearly in an example of a city so 'wrong' in every way it's hard to conceive of one worse.

Now a city, you might think, is *not* a person—body, soul and spirit. It's not a living entity. Such a thought only shows a tendency to categorise according to modern, western cultural mores. The cities of ancient times were queens, crowned with civic buildings, dressed in luxury, adorned with gardens.

It's easy to dismiss that image as a poetic metaphor. Except we don't know what *metaphor* meant back then.

And even so, if it is a metaphor, it points—as such lyric devices always do—to a deeper reality.

So let's accept this parallel between a city and a person. The particular city I have in mind got off on the wrong foot in every possible way. Yet God chose to restore her and to replace her wrecked cornerstone with a wondrous and perfect one. He made this city the jewel and centrepiece of His creation. She was, and is, Jerusalem.

It's so easy to picture her as she will be in the age to come, not as she was in ages past. The ideal can halo our image of her so naturally that we forget her early history shows no sign of promise. On the contrary, there are several despoiling aspects to her foundation that, humanly speaking, should have been disqualified her from any part in God's future plans for the salvation of Israel and the nations.

If I'd been a location scout for God's future blockbuster—the centuries-long spectacle featuring everything from the magnificent Temple of Solomon through beyond the resurrection of Jesus to His second coming—there's no way Jerusalem would ever have got a look in. I'd have instantly dismissed her from contention the moment I looked at her history and discovered her spiritual foundation was so utterly wretched.

We tend to avert our eyes from that rotten beginning. Yet, in fact, it's worth looking at because it's the greatest sign of hope imaginable for our own lives. God sees the glorious, unlimited potential in us—no matter how toxic our mess, how vile our background, how sick our souls.

I loved conferences. They were a chance to catch up with people I didn't see from one year to the next—a few days of intense connection followed by occasional letters or cards (yes, this was back in the days before email!) until the next annual get-together.

I bounced into one conference, a big smile on my face as I greeted an old friend from up north of the state. With a look half-glacial, half-venom, she turned away and stalked off. I stopped, not sure if I was the person she was reacting to or someone else nearby. Then, half a dozen people I knew well glanced my way, and deliberately turned their backs. It was so pointed it was impossible to miss. There were dozens of people there I corresponded regularly with, but none of them returned my greeting with their usual warmth and bright cheer. No one said a word. The frost was solid.

Eventually I found some vague acquaintances who were willing to say, 'Hello,' but none of them knew what was going on. I went away from the weekend, more puzzled than hurt. Sure I was upset, but the main feeling I had was *curiosity*. What was behind all the strange behaviour?

To this day, well over thirty years later, none of those friends who stopped speaking to me that day have ever made contact again. And I still don't know what it was about. But I do know who was responsible. I did some thinking about who *hadn't* spoken to me—and came to the conclusion that there was only one friend each of them had in common. The prime suspect therefore had to be my flatmate's best friend, Sonya.

It was difficult to believe: I would have sworn Sonya was a person of unimpeachable integrity. If she had a problem so deep with me that she had to share it with others, why didn't she speak to me first?

Now as it happened, Sonya came to visit my flatmate a couple of weeks after the conference. My flatmate was out. I was the only one home.

I knew the opportunity would never come again. And that I'd regret it all my life if I chickened out and didn't confront Sonya. So I told her what had happened, what I had concluded and asked her what she'd said and why she'd done it. I didn't say it angrily or nastily. I was shaking all over but managed to maintain my calm as I asked her for an explanation.

She stared at me, sadness in her eyes. 'Do you really think I would do something like this?'

I thought I could see tears. I almost apologised. *Almost.* I'm glad I didn't. I realised later that, in half an hour of conversation, she never once denied my accusation. And it's a normal response for innocent people to automatically deny an accusation. Over the years, I've come to realise that questions like, 'Do you really think I would do something like this?' or statements like, 'I thought you knew me better than that,' are huge red flags. All too often, they are not only indicators of a practitioner of abuse but a master manipulator.

I only realised this when I had approached a leader about a statement he'd made which had been taken the wrong way by an older woman, tormenting her greatly.

'I thought you knew me better than that,' he said when I explained her reaction. 'Do you really think that of me?'

I hesitated. It wasn't a comeback I'd anticipated. Somehow instead of the conversation being about a terrible and gaping communication hole, that I thought could be readily fixed, it had been turned on its head: it was all about *my* attitude. 'I think that it would be very easy to misinterpret your words and actions in this situation,' I told him. I was looking in his eyes as I said it and—to my surprise—I could see, from his reaction, I'd given the wrong answer. At least 'wrong' from the point of view that it was an answer he didn't want.

It took me years to understand why. In retrospect, I'd avoided a trap. The question, 'Do you really think that of me?' is designed to elicit a *yes* or *no* response. Moreover, it contained an implicit and subtle denial. It also deflected the problem straight back at me and tried to make me feel guilty for even thinking *maybe*, let alone *yes*. It basically and cleverly suggests, 'How could you possibly think someone of my integrity would stoop to dishonour? You're the one who is dishonouring others, not me.'

It didn't matter if I'd answered *yes* or *no*, either way it was an answer that can be controlled to the leader's advantage. If I'd answered *no*, of course, it would have defused any possible confrontation but it also meant I'd have had to immediately back off and side with the leader in the matter. Answering *yes*, on the other hand, would have meant I'd handed over the ammunition to him to claim I'd defamed him by calling his integrity into question. Not that he would have said that so bluntly—just implied it to his colleagues.

Deny, deflect, defame.

These are behaviours so like the classic pattern[3] of abuse—*deny, distract, reverse* victim and perpetrator—that they really can't be categorised as anything else. Yet this is not done with angry attack or furious bluster, it's done with a wounded smile and a sad question.

This particular leader had a reputation for standing up for victims of abuse—he was, yet again, someone I had the deepest respect for and believed was a person of impeccable integrity. It was many years before the way he operated in deceit and abuse was exposed. Unforgiveness, I believe, finally pushed him into becoming what he hated.

Master manipulators as both he and Sonya were, I'm sure neither of them was aware how damaging and abusive their behaviours were—they thought they were exactly the opposite. They thought of themselves as defenders of the abused, champions of the oppressed, advocates for the exploited and downtrodden.

I've also realised, in retrospect, that I've often been taken in by masks of integrity. Usually my discernment is quite reasonable, so I don't think this blindness is a coincidence. The spirit of abuse has a specialist tactic at its disposal—*group mind control*—and it's only those tiny light-splintered moments similar to that time I thought to yourself, 'That's not the answer he wanted to that question,' that we might begin to suspect we are failing to notice the obvious.

Every couple of weeks I chat with an expert who specialises in ministering to others about abuse. Originally a mutual friend recommended me to him because he was having difficulties crossing over his threshold into his destiny. I explained the importance of honour when it came to dealing with Leviathan. God upended his life, and that of his family, with just that simple key.

One week he mentioned he'd had a series of full-on sessions with several people who were all dealing with the devastation that comes from childhood physical abuse. 'They always say the same thing,' he remarked. 'Where was God?' He paused. 'That's not a question, it's an accusation.'

I had to agree.

Then he went on. 'You know, there's another thing everyone says, too. They say that the one good thing that has come out of their experience is that they know they can get through anything in life. They have survived. They have got through it. They have endured. These things always end.'

That thought eventually becomes a life statement: sooner or later, this will end. This too will pass. Behind it is the sneaking hope that I'm one day sooner to this trauma ending.

Sometimes, later in life, when abuse returns and begins to repeat itself and goes on and on, people begin to have quiet misgivings about their life statement. 'This will end' morphs into 'Will this ever end?' and perhaps even 'This will never end.'

'This will end' is a *false refuge*.

'Will this ever end?' is a *doubt*.

'This will never end' is a *lie*.

These thoughts don't necessarily have to be the result of extreme abuse. Disappointment on the threshold or extended suffering can plant them deep in our hearts.

All three—the false refuge, the doubt and the lie—are matters for repentance. Clinging to hope in the end of suffering, rather than the presence of God, is complicity with the enemy. How could God possibly be present, after all? The assumption behind that initial question, 'Why wasn't God there when I needed Him?' is that He abandoned us.

Now for several weeks before this conversation occurred I'd been suffering from an intensely painful rash on my face. I couldn't find any medication that would make a difference to the hot, gravelly skin condition. It was so bad it often disturbed my sleep. However, the following morning, in that half-way state between sleeping and waking, I touched my face and thought, 'It's starting to feel a bit better. It's just a matter of time until this is all over.'

Instantly I bolted upright, remembering the conversation I'd had the previous day and the words, 'It's simply a matter of time until the abuse is over,' and the conclusion that this was a false refuge.

I fled to God. 'This is how I deal with illness, isn't it? It's about time passing, about being one day closer to recovery, rather than You as the healer.' I was shocked at the discovery of my heart's deepest belief. 'Who have I got a covenant with?'

God was swift to answer. 'Time.'

I knew He wasn't talking about an abstraction. It was some sort of personified being, a dark spirit.[4] I thought about the old stories of Father Time—Kronos or Chronos, Saturn.[5] The child devourer—the elder-god so ravenous that he had to be chained beyond the end of the world lest he eat the present and future as well as the past.

I burst into tears. I wasn't standing against the ultimate abuser at all; I'd thought I was firm in my opposition to it but instead I was complicit with it. I was crushed by the knowledge of my own hypocrisy and duplicity. Yes, I knew quite well that the heart is deceitful and wicked above all things—after all, I'd unearthed quite a few false refuges in the past—but that doesn't make a new revelation of the heart's ongoing treachery towards God any less shattering. I sobbed for hours and, when I got over the worst of it, I said to God: 'I don't even know how to repent of this. Human beings are immersed in time—how do we not put some sort of hope in its passing? The temptation will always be right there, at our elbow.'

'You step into the eternal,' God said. 'You put your hope in Immanuel, *God with us*, and you seek His presence as He is present in the now.'

I've found this to be a relentless tension: a tug-of-war between Time and the Eternal. It's easy to see Time as a refuge—*Time heals all wounds*—and it's just as easy to see it as an abuser—*We feast on time as time feasts on us*.

The reason I've wanted to draw this 'face' of the spirit of abuse to your attention is because it's an aspect so easy to miss. When we're renouncing a covenant with Belial, it's essential to include Kronos as a side to its character. The names might seem completely different, yet in Babylon, Kronos was also known as Belus.[6]

Now it may not seem like Time has any connection with a cornerstone but, until we factor in the redeeming of time, we will miss a great deal of the Lord's guidance about overcoming abuse.

It was such a little lie.

So very little. It should never have borne such evil fruit. Other far bigger lies have blown up like powderpuffs and dissipated on the merest whiff of wind—but this tiny falsehood was different. It took me years to grasp what the distinctively different poison in its makeup was.

Our summer mission team was split into two sections: senior and junior. The senior team focussed on the northern campsite, the junior one on a caravan park at a southern beach locale. It was the junior team's night off and, together with two leaders I was training, we set off back to the main site to pick up the evening meal.

The cook presented us with a single lamb chop—raw—and a stalk of celery. We blinked in disbelief. She knew we had to feed fifteen people. But, seeing our shocked faces, she told us this was what she'd been informed we wanted.

I went to see the senior leader. There had been numerous communication breakdowns but this was the most serious yet. In fact, precisely because of the previous communication breakdowns, I'd several times checked to make sure he knew exactly what was required for the junior team's night off. We were supposed to be having a cheese fondue. It would force us to be together at one table and create the opportunity to pray for each others' stressload.

The senior leader was very apologetic. 'The fact is the team finances are gone. We just couldn't afford the expense.'

Suddenly the two trainees and I were the ones apologising. Abjectly. Grovellingly. 'If only we'd known, we wouldn't have troubled you,' we said, slinking off. Pooling our own meagre funds, we managed to buy some supplies at a local shop. But we knew it wasn't nearly enough.

We asked two team members if we could borrow some money. Naturally, they wanted to know why. So we explained. And word got round. Soon all the junior team knew the problem and, forming themselves into pairs and triplets, headed off in little hunter-gatherer groups to check out various stores.

In the end, it was a lovely evening—even better because we'd all contributed, all played a part in transforming disaster to success.

Two days later, it was the senior team's night off. The junior team arrived late because we were still finishing up our program. We couldn't believe our eyes when we walked into the dining hall—piles of fish and chips, mountains of burgers, crumbed sausages, battered scallops, buckets of fried chicken, salads, desserts, drinks. 'Dig in!' someone encouraged us. 'It's cook's night off and you can have whatever fast food you like.'

The entire junior team hesitated, holding back. None of us had any money. 'We can't pay,' I said.

'Don't worry about that!' our encourager exclaimed. 'It's free. It's been paid for from the team account.'

It was one of those moments when the air could have been cut with a knife. The junior team looked around and saw many, many, many hundreds of dollars of food spread out across the tables. And the leaders remembered the raw lamb chop and the stick of celery.

It was such a little lie: *the team finances are gone*.

But it destroyed everything. There was no junior team after that season.

Four years later, I woke up. Literally and figuratively. I hadn't thought of that summer mission for ages when, one morning, I opened my eyes from sleep and said aloud, 'It wasn't *my* fault.' I must have been dreaming about the mission. 'I'm 100% innocent. So why on earth have I believed for the last four years that I was 100% to blame?'

The 'junior team' had been a novel concept—it was to be a way of training up additional leaders under the umbrella of a larger team and accelerating their progress towards taking on a fully-fledged mission of their own. It went down in a ball of flames that year, never to be revived.

The senior leader responsible changed times, moved dates, altered programmes, rescheduled meetings and then failed to communicate those changes until the last moment. Oftentimes the junior team was by then committed to a publicly-advertised different activity. So the source of difficulty, disunity and disharmony always seemed to be the junior team—who were never there when work needed to be done.

All the problems arose because of **time**—and **timing**.

Despite the senior leader's example of forgiveness and tolerance, there was deep resentment in the wider team. They wouldn't have been human otherwise! The junior team was always missing-in-action—skipping out on the washing up, laundry duty, hall cleaning, rubbish collection, potato peeling, veggie preparation, tent erection, equipment setting up and dismantling, any and every dirty job.

Now forgiveness says this: the other person is in the wrong. The senior leader was effectively conveying the attitude that the junior team was the problem. He needed to repent and stop his habit of major last-minute changes or else take public responsibility for the damage and friction he was causing. Instead, his *deny-deflect-defame* was so subtle that it looked like *forgiveness* and *forbearance.*

But after four years, the evil fruit was obvious—crashes of faith, failure to raise up potential leaders, no other junior teams anywhere and thus no expansion of the ministry, a widespread belief amongst other leadership teams that junior teams were divisive and destructive.

I chose the adjective *evil* to describe the fruit with great intentionality. When I woke up that day, it was as if a thick blindfold had been abruptly lifted from my spiritual eyes and I said, 'That wasn't an ordinary run-of-the-mill bad lie. It was *evil*.' And then, immediately, I wondered what differentiated *evil* from *bad*.

So I set out on a quest to discover what the distinction was. Lots of investigation later, I ultimately concluded after reading Ted Peters' book, *Sin: Radical Evil in Soul and Society*, that real evil has to involve *inversion* of the good and the true. It isn't just something that's bad—it has to go beyond that. It has to *invert* the very idea of good and evil, replacing one with the other.

Did you spot the inversion in the story of the summer mission? I certainly didn't for a long time—not until I knew I should be looking for one.

This is a record of very low level abuse. From the start of my research into the spirit of abuse, I made the conscious decision to focus on small, under-the-radar incidents. There are many excellent books on major and high level abuse and I didn't want to reinvent the wheel. I wanted instead to hone in on those types of incidents when abuse was just sprouting and could potentially be nipped in the bud.

Abuse, by its nature, doesn't flower and fruit overnight— it's slow, slow, slow to ripen because it will never achieve the power over others that it craves if it is exposed early. It has to take its time to build an unassailable façade of integrity—so that *some* of the people can be fooled *all* of the time.

The most significant characteristic of the spirit of abuse is **inversion** or **perversion**. In fact, unless this aspect is present, then in my view it's doubtful this particular spirit is operating. Its signature scent is reversal of the holy.

There are any number of ways that the junior team could have discovered the lie about the overall finances, and none of them would have been as damaging as what actually occurred. That was because the inversion of a sacred symbol was involved. The very idea of a fondue, so very sixties and so completely outdated as it was, was a deliberate attempt to build unity. It was about prayer and fellowship—recognising that strangers living in close proximity in a stressful environment for a few weeks will necessarily find manners and habits in others that irritate them and get on their nerves. It was therefore about restoring peace and coming back into balance. And although this was not the original intention, it turned out to be a 'love feast' like the communion tables of the early church.

The lavish fast-food spread, on the other hand, fostered disunity. I'm sure that was not a conscious decision on the part of the overall leadership. However, the instructions were: take what you want, go where you want, be sure to be back before lights out. It's free time—go wherever you like and enjoy yourself.

So instead of togetherness, there was scattering. Instead of communion, there was separation and dispersal.

Both events were about meals: that is the most critical feature that creates the inversion. If they had been about different things, then symbol reversal would not have occurred. But because it did, and because it touched the very heart of the high priestly prayer that Jesus prayed at the Last Supper—that we all might be one with each other, with the Father and with Him—it had devastating and destructive power.

That is why it bore such evil fruit. It took that which was steeped in God's power—to love each other in truth and generosity—and turned that power back on itself to wreak destruction. It took acts of generous, even sacrificial, giving and made a mockery of them.

The key element in identifying the presence of the spirit of abuse is **inversion** or **perversion**. It has to be there. Yet other factors are also present. The other signature smell when it comes to this spirit is **group mind control.**

This is not the same as individual mind control or mesmerism which is a specialty of the spirit of Leviathan. In that instance, individuals are each affected separately and in different ways while their friends are repeatedly stunned by how oblivious they are to the obvious. But with **group mind control**, the opposite is the case. A few individuals remain unaffected but the group as a whole is asleep. They fail to notice anything wrong, no matter how blatant it is. And the group becomes very annoyed, even combative, if any attempt is made to waken them. They don't want to hear the other side of the story; they don't even want to hear that there is another side.

A third element—although this is not unique to the spirit of abuse, as **inversion** and **group mind control** are—is **blame-shifting**.

What is different with abuse, however, is that victims tend to accept blame without demur. Scapegoating is a tactic of Azazel, the spirit of rejection—but those subjected to that spirit's torment don't fail to notice it. They may not openly kick and push against the scapegoating but they definitely know they've been unjustly accused. The same is not true when dealing with the spirit of abuse: in this scenario, those afflicted may not even be aware of their own innocence. Guilt has been induced in them to such a degree they believe they are responsible, even when they are not. The truth has been twisted so far it's bent back on itself.

When I woke up after four years and spoke to the trainee leaders, discovering that they—like me—had blamed themselves, I couldn't initially convince them they were not at fault. Not in any way, shape or form. Not for several more years. They excused the senior leader, constantly rationalising his actions and flipping his responsibility onto themselves.

By the time they did wake up, it was so long after the event it seemed pointless doing anything much about what happened. Except forgive.

Time.

Again.

Yes, this is another variation on the 'time passing' weapon that the spirit of abuse deploys against us. Coupled with group mind control, it is a delaying and disabling tactic that cripples and immobilises us until it's too late. All too often victims do nothing, for a lifetime, because in their eyes too much time has passed for any good to come of bringing the matter up and exposing the perpetrator. For many people it's only if and when they see the abuser using the same tactics on others that they decide to take their secret out of hiding.

Then, all too often, they are engaged in an uphill battle to be believed by family or community members who remain loyal to the abuser. Or if the accusers are in fact believed, then they find fingers are pointed at them for being unforgiving—once again switching the responsibility for sin from abuser to victim, trying to induce shame in the innocent rather than the guilty and losing sight of both real mercy and genuine justice.

Before going further, I want to make clear that there are different categories of ill-treatment. It's all too easy to lump them into one bulging box labelled 'abuse'. However, when I am discussing 'abuse' in this book I am specifically referring to the kind of harm that results from a desire for **power over others**. Molestation or exploitation automatically fall into this group, but other behaviours may not. Yet, if the end goal of violence or neglect is *having control over others*, then they too join this category.

You're welcome to define it differently, but for the purposes of this book, my narrow focus is behaviour that is primarily motivated by a desire for power and control. Any discussion of Belial, spirit of abuse, uses this as a criterion. As you'll have discovered if you've read other books in this series, the threshold spirits are multi-faceted and several-faced. Yet there is a tendency in spiritual warfare to attribute just one function to a spirit—a spirit of anger or a spirit of lust or a spirit of fear—when it's far from that simple. Just as people are complex personalities and not driven by a single emotion, neither are spirits. The spirit of abuse is also a spirit of armies. Moreover, as we've already seen, one of its other faces is Kronos, spirit of time.

As well as recognising the complex nature of spirits and thus, often, that we're not afflicted by a wild multitude of them but just one, it's also important to discern between spirits. Because not every episode of violence is necessarily about the spirit of abuse.

One incident stands out in my childhood memories. My father was laminating a table-top and just as he'd nearly finished, a large bubble formed he simply couldn't remove. He yelled in frustration, drawing everyone's attention. His rage was uncontrollable. He lashed out and hit anyone who tried to help—and, for decades thereafter, every time he exhibited anger, some members of my family saw abuse.

One day, after many years, I was surprised when one of them said my dad was abusive. I defended him and said I didn't recall him that way at all. When various incidents were brought up to support the accusation, I said I thought differently. It wasn't that those events didn't happen—they did. However I recalled my dad as a perfectionist who, if something went wrong, would become violently angry at himself for not getting the job done exactly right. He refused to pay anyone to do anything he could do himself and he demanded an exacting professional level of himself even when he'd never tackled a particular task before. In addition, because he was afraid of rejection, he wouldn't ask for help and then, when he really needed it and he couldn't manage by himself, he would work himself into such a towering fury it was best to stay right out of his way.

Realising even as a small girl that it was not about anger at me but anger at himself, I'd always removed myself from the vicinity for a couple of hours until he calmed down.

The reactions to my explanation were interesting. What others had seen until that moment as abuse directed against themselves they now agreed was really violence directed at himself. He was punishing himself.

Sure, different family members had been afraid and traumatised but, as they mentally went over various incidents, they could see immediately that none of them were about attaining power over anyone else: they were all about internal rage at not being perfect. Underneath it all was a bed-rock of self-rejection, built on a cornerstone of his mother's rejection of her pregnant condition, her panic at finding herself expecting a child while unmarried and her attempts to hide the baby growing in her womb by fasting so she would not put on weight.

Rejection is the territory of Azazel. It's the spirit of rejection and panic, scapegoating and lust. It's important to recognise that the way to overcome Azazel is completely different from the method of dealing with Belial or Kronos. These spirits—rejection and abuse—can of course work together but it is worth distinguishing their different modes of defilement.

Ask the Holy Spirit which threshold spirit you are facing because the rules of engagement differ. If you've read *Dealing with Python*, you'll know it's love as a Fruit of the Spirit that works best against the constrictor. And if you've read *Dealing with Ziz*, you'll know it's joy as a Fruit of the Spirit that works best against the raptor. And if you've read *Dealing with Leviathan* or *Dealing with Resheph*, you'll know it's peace—shalom—as a Fruit of the Spirit that overcomes the retaliators. For Azazel, it's self-control—better translated as spirit-empowerment.

Each of these Fruit are spiritual in nature, not fleshly. Unless we have allowed the Holy Spirit to ripen *His* variety of Fruit in us through testing and trial, the carnal versions inevitably fail. Peace—*shalom*—for example, is developed by building integrity. This only comes through facing challenges where we've been seriously tempted to be dishonest, manipulative or underhanded. We can't claim to have genuine diamond-lustre integrity until we've passed through the crushing pressure and the relentless minefire of those tests—until we've kept our word even though it was seriously to our disadvantage to do so, until we've stared ruin in the face and turned down a shady opportunity that would save us, until we're fronting up to a grim situation for the second time and the cost of truth in the first instance broke us emotionally and spiritually.

Yet, of ourselves, we can never attain or keep integrity. Only Jesus can hold it for us, only He can keep it safe for us. If we fail these tests, and some of them are brutal, the Fruit simply doesn't ripen to form armaments against the power of the enemy of our souls. It may wither away or simply stagnate in an arrested state of development.

Way back in the Garden of Eden, fruit was weaponised against humanity. Now, the reverse is true. This is because one of the most basic principles embedded within the design of creation is the 'law of action-reaction'—sometimes called 'sowing-and-reaping'. Almost every society knew of it spiritually long before Isaac Newton discovered the third law of motion in physics: *for every action, there is an equal and opposite reaction.*

Some cultures called it 'karma', some said, 'What goes around, comes around,' some refer to it as 'cause-and-effect'.

Now it doesn't just apply on the human plane. It also applies in the heavenlies. Just as we sow and reap, so does our enemy. Fruit was weaponised by the devil, so Fruit can now be weaponised against him. Consequently the Fruit of the Spirit, when tested and tried, can be arrayed for use in defeating the threshold spirits. In fact, the fully tested and mature Fruit of the Spirit are peerless and practical weapons, providing we can identify which spirit we're facing and therefore which of the Fruit needs to be deployed.

All this may be a surprise if you're used to thinking of the Fruit of the Spirit in elementary Sunday School terms as simply about character formation. Absolutely it's about character formation: it's about the making of a warrior. A warrior who carries weapons that can never be lost or laid aside—because they are carried within ourselves. They become part of who we are.

We can surrender these weapons. We can choose the fruit of the flesh—

> *sexual immorality, impurity, and debauchery; idolatry and sorcery; hatred, discord, jealousy, and rage; rivalries, divisions, factions, and envy; drunkenness, orgies.*
>
> Galatians 5:19–21 BSB

But Jesus is here to empower us to overcome the temptations and pass the tests.

It's very easy to dismiss the Fruit as kiddie stuff—nice, but sometimes almost a liability in life's battleground. Certainly not like the adult stuff of being an apostle, prophet, pastor, evangelist, teacher. And not like the spectacularly visible gifts of prophecy, tongues, interpretation, miracle-working, discernment of spirits or healing either.

Yet Jesus didn't say His disciples would know each other by their gifts or their offices. We forget His heart-breaking words about prophets and miracle-workers:

> *'By their fruit you will recognise them. Not everyone who says to Me, "Lord, Lord," will enter the kingdom of heaven, but only the one who does the will of My Father who is in heaven. Many will say to Me on that day, "Lord, Lord, did we not prophesy in Your name and in Your name drive out demons and in Your name perform many miracles?" Then I will tell them plainly, "I never knew you. Away from Me, you evildoers!"'*
>
> Matthew 7:20–23 NIV

There's a very good reason for this: the gifts are just that—*gifts*. God doesn't ever ask for them back. If He did, they wouldn't be gifts. They'd be tools on loan.

Because they are irrevocable, and not given as a reward for performance but as an award of grace, they are not an indicator of kingdom status. But we tend to default into thinking that way and become perplexed when God does not withdraw His gift of healing from a minister living in adultery or retrieve His gift of evangelism from a person engaged in deep fraud.

The reason is simple: it's a *gift*.

To know our brothers and sisters in Christ, we should look for evidence of the Fruit of the Spirit, not His gifts.

Prayer

Heavenly Father, help. Please help. I need to deal with me first, but my discernment is so shattered and scattered it's possible I'm actually as needy as those I see abusing others.

I don't know if a hood has been pulled over my mind. I'm not aware of it, yet how would I know, if it's so subtle? I'm not sure if I have ever given other people the kind of trust I should only ever grant to You. Have I been conned by sly words that suggest integrity: 'Do you really think that of me?' 'Do you honestly believe I would do something like that?' 'Don't you know me better than that?' Help me to know if I've been caught in a snare and not even realised it.

Lord, I find myself at a loss what to say when I'm trying to resolve a painful problem. Instead of a dialogue, I realise the discussion has so often been deflected and diverted into questions about my trust, my loyalty and my allegiance to the person I'm confronting. Instead of addressing their own actions, they flip the conversation and want to examine my attitude. And then I plunge myself into guilt for even doubting their uprightness of heart. The hood over my eyes thickens by another layer.

I don't even know how many blindfolds are over my eyes. I ask You, through the power of the redeeming blood of

Jesus, to rip off all the veils and hoods that blind me to the activity and influence of the spirit of abuse. Tear away the mind control over me. Give me a right sense of responsibility to know what I am accountable for and what others are accountable for. Show me where I have believed myself to be at fault when, in fact, I have been mostly or even entirely innocent.

Lord, my willingness to accept blame is complicity with the spirit of abuse. I confess that I have sided with it, and I repent of that back-to-front way of dealing with its influence. I repent of allowing the hood to be placed over my mind. I repent of asking, 'Where was God in all this?' and so accusing You with that very question of not being there for me. I repent of putting my faith in Time or in the passing of Time as my healer, my saviour and my refuge. I renounce any covenants with Time—under any of its names—or with the Hooded One, whatever it may be called, or with blindness or with the thief of vision, whether physical or spiritual. I ask Jesus of Nazareth to empower the words of repentance and renunciation I have just spoken.

Lord, I recognise that the group mind control exercised by the spirit of abuse is a perversion of the oneness of covenant. It's assimilation, rather than incorporation into a Body. It's sameness, rather than diverse graces coupled together as unity. It's a 'hive mind', rather than the varied flows and breezes of Your Holy Spirit with all His varied modes of confirmation and insight. I repent of the times

I quenched the Voice of Your Holy Spirit and listened to the lies of the spirit of abuse. I repent of not asking You what the truth was when all the tactics of denial, deflection and defamation were in operation. I just got so confused. Please remind me, when I am confused, to run to You and ask for help. Again, I ask Your Son, Jesus Christ, the redeemer of the world and of time, to take my words and make them powerful and effective to achieve the mindchange I so desperately need.

In His holy name. Amen.

3
Stealing Healing

From time to time I'm going to repeat myself in this book. The reason is simple. One of the tactics of the spirit of abuse is to repeat a lie so often that we believe it. Even the most blatant and outrageous contradictions settle in our minds as truth. In our confusion, we decide on an external authority to help guide us—and, almost invariably, we make the worst possible choice in this regard. We need to choose someone loyal to the truth and to God, but we usually choose someone who will do everything to minimise conflict and maintain the reputation of the organisation they represent.

So, to the first repetition. The tactics of the spirit of abuse include:

- **inversion** or **perversion** of **symbols**
- **group mind control**
- **blame-shifting**
- **time-wasting** or **time-passing**

I'm initially focusing on these because most of them are almost universally overlooked. I've categorised them in slightly different ways because I want to look at a more general application than other writers.

One common tactic mentioned by many counsellors is the tendency of abusers and their supporters to ***reverse the victim and perpetrator.*** Abusers reframe their stories in such a way that they present themselves as the real wounded in the situation. The truth is, they are genuinely damaged people who can believe their own lies—and their seeming veracity can influence others to believe them too. Nevertheless, this type of reversal is just one aspect of a wider symptom: the **inversion** or **perversion** of symbols.

Another common tactic is ***gaslighting***—making up false and misleading stories that cause selected others to doubt their own perceptions. About a week after my dad's funeral, my mother became troubled that she hadn't heard from one of his closest colleagues. Fearing the person may have had an accident, she made a phone call—only to be more disturbed afterwards than she had been before. 'Am I going mad?' she asked. The colleague had described my dad's funeral in detail, commented on the eulogy, mentioned others who'd been there. My mother was genuinely distressed by the conversation because she concluded, after getting off the phone, that she must have coldly ignored this colleague at the funeral.

'No!' I had to say to her. 'It's not true! And you're not going mad. I remember exactly who was at the funeral. Do you want me to get out the attendance record to prove it?'

Had I not absolutely, vehemently, repeatedly assured my mother that her memory was spot-on, she would have been back on the phone within minutes apologising for rudeness that she'd never dished out. It was a small lie on the part of dad's colleague but it revealed an ability to mentally rewrite history and present it with such dexterous sincerity that an apology was never seen to be needed—instead the person being gaslit was almost manipulated into believing she needed to offer one!

Gaslighting is simply one aspect of a much wider tactic: **group mind control**. The overarching agenda behind this is to get everyone to buy into the lie. On the one hand, some people are targeted by gaslighting to question their own reality, and on the other hand, by-standers are induced to believe falsehoods simply by the repetition of the dominant narrative, however inconsistent it is.

The **group mind control** is an essential steppingstone to building an army. This, after all, is another face of the spirit of abuse: it is also a spirit of **armies**. Now of course it's necessary for an army to obey orders without question and without hesitation. So, any attempt at dialogue, any request for an explanation of contradictory elements, any comment asking for clarification, is instantly blocked. Or deflected.

It's important to recognise that, when we are dealing with people influenced by the spirit of abuse, there is an **army** commander of the spirit world behind them. And that cosmic general is furious we have not recognised his status, jumped instantly to attention and obeyed without demur. We have dared to doubt the messaging of the propaganda machine behind him. And so the disinformation increases: the denials, deflections, defamation, distortion and distraction go into overdrive. And now of course it may include us, simply because *we asked questions*.

For many years after I had confronted Sonya that day my flatmate was out, I was desperate to know what she'd said. I wasn't ever angry. I was far too bewildered to reach that emotion. I couldn't even begin to imagine what she'd said. What could possibly be so bad that so many people never spoke to me again? What could possibly be *so bad* that no one was willing to ask me about it and try to ascertain whether it was true or not?

About three years later, I was talking to a friend who happened to mention that two of my close friends had fallen out over Sonya's allegations. I hadn't known of that further incident previously. Glenda had apparently said to Karyn, her very best friend: 'It's Anne or me. You choose. You can't stay friends with us both.' Karyn had replied, 'I've known Anne decades longer than I've known you. I don't believe this.' And so, keeping her word, Glenda severed her friendship with Karyn.

This was the moment when I finally realised, beyond any shadow of a doubt, that Sonya's question, 'Do you really think I would do something like that?' was a diversionary tactic, not an implicit denial. I'd been almost entirely certain that was the case, but I still retained the slimmest of slim hopes I was wrong and that I'd misinterpreted her words as evasion when they were really a cry of the heart. What if I'd accused an innocent person? Perhaps she was still the person of integrity I'd once believed her to be.

The friend who was telling me all this went on to say that Glenda and Karyn had made up about ten months later, once Glenda finally woke up to the realisation that 'something was very wrong in Sonya's head.'

It was my opportunity to find out the facts: I asked my friend what Sonya had said. His expression seized up, and his eyes reminded me of a rabbit caught in headlights. In all our talk, he hadn't realised I didn't know the background. 'I don't remember,' he gulped. And after a few mild efforts to penetrate that abrupt loss of memory, I let him be.

But I added another question to my *so-bad* list: What could be *so bad* that one woman would deliver an ultimatum to her best friend *and then actually carry out the threat*, all because that friend refused to give up a longstanding friendship with me?

I had a good argument that I persistently presented to God. I *need* to know, I told Him, so I can forgive Sonya. A vague hand-wave of forgiveness, lacking in specificity, hardly cuts it as a genuine pardon. Besides that, I said, trying to bolster my case, because I don't know what it's all about, I don't actually know if I did something I need to apologise for and repent of. There may be fault on both sides. I simply *don't know*. Many dozens of people are aware of exactly what happened, I informed Him—surely one of them is willing to talk.

But time has passed, and no one ever has.

The activity of Kronos—the particular face of the spirit of abuse related to **Time**—is never more evident than when we get stuck in the moment of trauma. We speak in the past tense, rather than the present. When we've been abused or mistreated, we tell the same story over and over. Or alternatively we search to find out *why* and make sense of the confusion we feel. The past is not in its rightful place. The past is present—and tries to consume it.

Kronos, the spirit of Time, presents us with a counterfeit of eternity. Instead of Immanuel's presence in the *now*, we experience the moment of trauma as *now*. And because our question, 'Where was God in all this?' means we've already discarded the possibility He was at work for us, our false refuge is 'reliving the scene'.

I asked God over and over to direct someone to me who was willing to reveal what Sonya said. And I kept at Him and at Him and at Him until the day I read Tim Winton's novel, *The Riders*.

I have a love-hate relationship with Tim Winton's writing. His works are peppered with profanity but some are profound, while some belong to that rare category of books I'd be prepared to fling on a bonfire.

Let me spoil the plotline of *The Riders* for you. Fred Scully and his wife, Jennifer, spend two years in Europe before buying a cottage in Ireland. She goes back to Australia to sell their home and pack their belongings while he sets about renovating the cottage of her dreams. Some months later, he waits at an airport arrival gate, eager to be reunited with Jennifer and their seven-year-old daughter, Billie.

His life goes into freefall when Billie steps off the plane but his wife does not. She's disappeared. Apparently, at the last stopover, she shepherded Billie onto a flight then stayed behind.

Scully is desperate to know what happened and why. Where is Jennifer? Why has his daughter lost the power of speech? What trauma has she suffered? How did he not know his marriage was in dire trouble? Why would Jennifer leave without a word of explanation? His mind runs over the events of the last few years looking for clues that might explain events—but they elude him. He begins a journey across Europe with Billie in an attempt to track his wife down.

One evening, in Ireland, Scully wakes up and walks across the fields to a ruined castle. There, in a surreal and dream-like landscape, he sees a shadowy group of riders, dressed in ancient armaments and lit by flaming torches. A supernatural, numinous aura surrounds them. He walks among them but they do not see him.

This short scene gives the book its title. It is an enigmatic, otherworldly interlude in the novel. Many readers find it unsettling and incongruous. It's a momentary supernatural blip in an otherwise gut-wrenching psychological mystery. For many people, it undermines the question posed by the story, 'How well can we *really* know another person?'

By the end of the novel, however, Scully's vision of the Riders recurs. His great moment of choice revolves around a realisation of their identity and, with that, his recognition of his own danger. His desire to *know* has become obsessional and destructive. He can pursue it, a quest without end, just as the restless spirits of the Riders continue to chase their unfulfilled 'dues' across countless centuries during their recurrent night-journeys.

He can surrender the desire to know. Or he can continue on and ultimately join the Riders.

When I finished this book, I realised God was asking me to surrender the desire to know what Sonya had said and why. Giving up the *why* was the hardest. But God turned the *why* back on me. *Why do you want to know?* He asked. *Is it really about forgiveness or is it because you want to assure yourself you are innocent and can be vindicated?*

Honestly, I can't answer that question. I think it's a mixture of both.

But, even having God pull me up on my motives, I don't believe He was suggesting I was wrong to want to know. The moment we are asked to take sides, we cannot offer anyone the sort of trust and loyalty that is due only to God. In a Christian context, we need to be aware that, when we're asked to take sides, we are being positioned to *judge* between believers—and acting as just judges is part of everyone's calling. We need to exercise that office with impartiality and wisdom. Since we're commanded in Scripture to honour everyone, we need to be cautious about leaping to defend someone when we've only heard their side of the story.

For over ten years, one of my neighbours would regularly confide in me about her abusive husband. I never had any reason to doubt her word. Then one day she rang and asked if I could come over and see him. I was the only person she knew, so she said, who could talk about spiritual things. Her husband, an atheist, was deeply troubled. He was being followed by a spirit.

He'd seen it, she'd seen it. He'd finally become alarmed enough to talk about it openly when it had manifested in his workplace and his colleagues started to comment with nudges and winks on the 'woman' who followed him everywhere.

The ensuing conversation was a salutary lesson. He described the spirit and because it sounded like a valkyrie, I asked him if he'd been in the military. It transpired he'd been a commissioned officer—and had fought in Vietnam and Africa. I said I'd heard rumours, but had never been able to substantiate them, about spirits stalking battlefields in Vietnam, choosing those who were to die, like the valkyries of Norse legend. I didn't have an Asian name for them, but in other cultures they would be termed 'deathbringers' or 'wishmaidens' or 'psychopomps'.

Both the man and his wife nodded immediately. They knew exactly what I was talking about. Our conversation moved on and the woman began to point out her husband's shortcomings. To my surprise, he admitted them. That was the first sign the stories of abuse I'd heard were vastly more complicated than I'd been led to believe. He wasn't doing the typical *deny, deflect, defame* routine—but he did say that his wife's problems were not really with him but with her parents. Maybe that was *blame-shifting* but I wasn't sure, particularly when he agreed he had been very harsh with his wife in the past but he was sincerely endeavouring to change. Nor did his admission seem like it was an overture in the art of love-bombing, a part of the sweet-mean cycle with its intermittent reinforcement that brings on a state very much like Stockholm Syndrome. It's part of a psychological warfare routine that, over time, conditions the victim to accept more abuse and less affection. Time, yet again, being used against us to boost trauma and amplify its effects across generations.

As we continued the conversation, my neighbour's husband steadfastly maintained that his wife projected her parents' behaviour onto him. I wondered if he'd actually nailed the root issue. A common cause of problems in life is that we've judged our parents, secretly condemned them, and so we are unable to reap the benefits of obeying the commandment to honour our parents. Life has not gone well with us.

I explained the spiritual law of sowing-and-reaping in terms of unforgiveness to my neighbours and the husband got it at once. The wife didn't. That was startling: the atheist grasped the principle but the Christian didn't.

So I asked for some specific examples of projection from him. It quickly became obvious that what was unforgiveable behaviour in him was, according to his wife, not only forgiveable in her parents—it was a non-issue. She was angry at the suggestion her parents needed to be forgiven. It didn't matter how her parents treated her: it was fine coming from them. However, if her husband acted in a similar way, she had grounds for divorce.

She could recognise that the very qualities she admired in her father were what drew her to her husband in the first place. However, she couldn't see into her own heart and admit that what she secretly hated in her father was precisely what she openly loathed in her husband. The inexorable law of sowing-and-reaping had drawn her into a marriage where unforgiveness brought about a replay of the early abuse. She was complicit with that spirit—both through her inability to forgive her parents and her hidden judgment that they had abused her. She believed she was honouring her parents when, in fact, she was *guilty* of condemning them.

This is *not to say* that the husband was innocent. Nor to exonerate him in any way. It is to say, however, that his efforts at changing were defiled by his wife's unforgiveness and hypocrisy. Moreover, she had abdicated her position as her husband's armour-bearer and paraclete. And it had been taken by a valkyrie-like spirit she'd been acquainted with since her childhood in Asia.

It was a much more complex situation than I'd been led to believe over our decade of chatting together. Both partners were influenced by the spirit of abuse—the husband to perpetrate it; the wife to be complicit with it. She'd believed the lie the spirit had told her that forgiving her parents was dishonouring them; when, in reality, it would have been honour. She had become so deeply enmeshed in the idea of being the victim it never dawned on me to question her story of being one of the 'boat people'—a refugee who'd arrived, poverty-stricken and visa-less, after a traumatic sea journey to the northern shores of Australia on a crowded, rickety boat.

Her husband was incensed when she repeated this claim during the conversation. 'You are *not!*' he snapped. 'I brought you to Australia on a plane.'

'I *identify* with boat people!' she screamed back at him.

One of my brothers joked recently at a party that, because his wife treated her dogs so well, he had decided to come 'out of the closet'. From then on, the family was to understand that he identified as an Italian greyhound, and to cuddle and feed him accordingly. I told him he was making a huge mistake. 'You don't say, "I *identify* as an Italian greyhound," but "I *am* an Italian greyhound." There's a big difference.'

And the difference is not apparent until we have enough information to challenge a victim status. Only then is 'I *identify*' trotted out as a justification for a deception. This is appropriation of victimhood, whether it involves the Stolen Generations or Boat People or survivor of cruelty of any kind. Such appropriation is abuse in its own right. It demeans the genuine victims, exploits their stories, ravages the truth and constitutes an agreement with the spirit of abuse.

The **perversion** of language—and particularly symbols—is symptomatic of the presence of the spirit of abuse. Each of the threshold guardians plays with truth in a slightly different way. But the spirit of **abuse, armies, time** and **group mind control** wants to convince us that black is white and white is black and there is no such thing as grey.

It's worth pausing for a moment to look at the different ways the threshold guardians handle truth.

Python, the spirit of constriction, hides the truth in a riddle or an ambiguity. There are no outright falsehoods but double meanings will abound.

Ziz, the spirit of forgetting, tears the truth apart. This can be through false accusation, or simply a failure to accurately recall events or possibly even a mental rearrangement of an episode in our personal history to ensure we're always the hero in our own stories.

Leviathan, the spirit of retaliation, twists and distorts the truth, sliding off at a tangent whenever clarification is sought, and causing misunderstanding or misinterpretation.

Azazel, the spirit of rejection, manipulates and downgrades truth so it is seen as unimportant. Values such as harmony, acceptance and tolerance are regarded as more important.

Lilith, the vampiric spirit, weaponises truth and upgrades it so it is more important than love or grace or peace.

Rachab, the spirit of wasting, portrays truth as relative and private. There is no absolute truth, just a personal perspective on it. All viewpoints are considered equally valid.

Belial, the spirit of abuse, perverts and inverts truth so that evil is seen as good.

There are many names other than Belial that identify the spirit of abuse. Each of them highlights a different facet of this spirit's make-up. Belial is the name that occurs most often in Scripture; Kronos emphasises its role in using time against us; the Janissary—a title I used in my earlier writings—indicates it is a spirit of armies with an agenda of turning children against their parents.

Once however we realise this spirit specialises in reversing good and evil, we can also name it as Beelzebul. Look at the incident where Jesus is accused of being in league with the satan:

> *Then they brought him a demon-possessed man who was blind and mute, and Jesus healed him, so that he could both talk and see. All the people were astonished and said, 'Could this be the Son of David?'*
>
> *But when the Pharisees heard this, they said, 'It is only by Beelzebul, the prince of demons, that this fellow drives out demons.'*

Jesus knew their thoughts and said to them, 'Every kingdom divided against itself will be ruined... If Satan drives out Satan, he is divided against himself. How then can his kingdom stand? And if I drive out demons by Beelzebul, by whom do your people drive them out? So then, they will be your judges. But if it is by the Spirit of God that I drive out demons, then the kingdom of God has come upon you... And so I tell you, every kind of sin and slander can be forgiven, but blasphemy against the Spirit will not be forgiven. Anyone who speaks a word against the Son of Man will be forgiven, but anyone who speaks against the Holy Spirit will not be forgiven, either in this age or in the age to come.'

Matthew 12:22–37 NIV

Prior to Jesus' ministry, many traditions had sprung up about how the Messiah could be identified. There was a belief in a royal messiah, the Son of David; a war messiah, the Son of Joseph; the priestly messiah, after the order of Melchizedek; and the Elijah-who-was-to-come. One of the signs by which the Son of David could be identified would be His ability to cast out demons, particularly deaf and dumb ones. Jewish priests had rites of exorcism for demons but they involved acquiring power over it through naming it. Getting a demon to name itself was impossible if it was dumb.

So when the people asked, *'Could this be the Son of David?',* what they were really wondering was: 'Could this be the royal messiah?' When the Pharisees insisted the answer was 'no' by slandering Jesus, their accusations were multi-pronged. They implied that the healing Jesus performed was diabolic in nature; that His ministry belonged to the darkness, not to the light; that people loyal to Yahweh should flee from Jesus because He was allied with the Lord's enemies; that it was a delusion to see the work of God in what was obviously hell-inspired activity; that He could not possibly be any of the expected messiahs because He was an ambassador of the prince of demons.

As a consequence of equating the power of the Holy Spirit with satanic control, the Pharisees were basically saying that good was evil. They would have caused many who might have sought help from Jesus to avoid Him. It was better, apparently, in their view to be possessed by a deaf and mute demon than to be healed and freed by Jesus.

Nothing much has changed in the last two millennia. It's common for people who've been subjected to satanic ritual abuse to have been deliberately introduced to a false Jesus so that they are triggered into panicked flight by the real Jesus of Nazareth. They've been brainwashed into believing that the Lord of infinite compassion and healing is evil and depraved. They've been deprived of all possibility of comfort and consolation because the signs and symbols of God are associated in their minds with intense trauma and the vilest of abuse.[7]

This is the sin against the Holy Spirit: stealing healing from God's beloved children by convincing them that good is corrupt, wicked, deviant and foul. By persuading them blessings are curses, and curses are blessings. By inducing them to believe that good is evil, and evil is good—and that love is necessarily about cruelty, and that abuse is a form of affection.

There's always brainwashing of some form involved. Indoctrination, programming, conditioning, grooming —mind control, characterised by inversions and perversions that bear the stamp of the sin against the Holy Spirit. This results in near-total blindness when it comes to the Fruit of the Spirit: love, joy, peace, patience, kindness, goodness, faithfulness, gentleness and self-control. Love is presented as 'hate' and joy as 'mockery'; peace is portrayed as 'injustice' and patience as 'playing for time'; kindness, goodness and faithfulness are labelled 'violence', gentleness 'insensitivity' and self-control 'conformity'.

As mentioned previously, each of the threshold spirits is overcome by a particular Fruit of the Spirit. Can you tell which is effective against Belial from the list above? It's the combination of goodness, kindness and faithfulness—which, in Hebrew, is one single and very beautiful concept, 'chesed'. The archaic word, *lovingkindness*,[8] is sometimes used to translate it but even that doesn't capture its entire range of nuances.

Now, if you've been subjected to serious abuse in your life and you don't immediately question the last paragraph, it's time to pray a lot more earnestly about the lifting of mind control in your life. If you don't automatically think to yourself that my statement that 'chesed'—goodness, kindness and faithfulness as the key to overcoming abuse—is a hopeless trivialisation or a damaging simplification, you need genuine and professional help.

By themselves, goodness, kindness and faithfulness are going to be smashed, pulled inside out and presented to the watching world by the abuser as malice, cruelty and betrayal. Before the Fruit can be actually effective, you need the right *cornerstone*. Your damaged, defiled and fractured foundation simply isn't up to stockpiling 'chesed' in the storerooms of your life. Goodness, kindness and faithfulness are going to slip through the cracks every time.

The answer to this issue of the right foundation is simple: you need Jesus, the Chief Cornerstone, as your own personal cornerstone.

Before we look more closely at what that entails, I want to make a monumentally important point. When it comes to the spirit of abuse—a threshold guardian—there are always **choices**. We can sometimes become so confused and disoriented we don't believe that. The confusion is often exacerbated by well-meaning counsellors who insist that believers must reconcile with the abuser, particularly when a spouse is involved. Never forget that the spirit of abuse specialises in **group mind control** and even the best of counsellors can fall prey to it.

Now I shouldn't have to say this because Scripture is very clear. **No. We don't have to reconcile.** We can choose to separate ourselves entirely—and this is, in fact, the course of action recommended by the Word of God. The Lord does not require us to put ourselves in harm's way.

Reconciliation has two parts: *forgiveness* and *repentance*. The victim is called to *forgive*; the perpetrator to *repent*. If one forgives but the other fails to repent, there can be no reconciliation. Likewise, if one repents and the other fails to forgive, there can be no reconciliation.

Even if both forgiveness and repentance occur, there needs to be a period of **time** in which *goodness, kindness* and *faithfulness* are repeatedly demonstrated by both parties before close relationship can be rightly re-established. **Time** has been used *against* us, now it must be used *for* us. And when children have been abused, there can be no limitation on the time of separation.

The reason counsellors do not recognise the Scriptural injunction allowing separation is because they do not identify the spirit of abuse as Belial. They therefore do not understand the following words from Paul:

> *What do righteousness and wickedness have in common? Or what fellowship can light have with darkness? What harmony is there between Christ and Belial? Or what does a believer have in common with an unbeliever? What agreement*

is there between the temple of God and idols? For we are the temple of the living God. As God has said... 'Come out from them and be separate.'

2 Corinthians 6:14–17 NIV

This is the only time Belial is mentioned in the epistles or gospels. It is, however, mentioned twenty-seven times in Hebrew. *Twenty-seven!* However English versions generally skim right over it by translating the name Belial as *worthless* or *wicked*. This slide into an abstraction means the connection to idol worship is erased.

Belial is a malign cosmic commander-in-chief, the very spirit that in the time of Jesus was considered the ultimate arch-enemy of God. It has been hidden from sight in most modern translations by being transformed into a bad character trait. Belial must be laughing obscenely at having pulled off such a masterful coup.

Belial is first mentioned in Deuteronomy. God revealed that complicity with this spirit brought about a defilement of both **land** and **people**. He then told the people how they were to deal with such arcane darkness in the future.

> *You may hear in one of your towns that the Lord your God is giving you to inhabit that worthless men [**sons of Belial**] have come from among you to entice those who live in the towns. They*

may say, 'Let's go and serve other gods that you haven't known.'

You must thoroughly investigate and inquire if it is true that this detestable thing exists among you. If it is so, then put the inhabitants of the town to death by the sword. Devote everything in it to divine destruction—even its livestock—by the sword... burn the town... It will remain a permanent mound of ruins, never to be rebuilt again.

Deuteronomy 13:12–16 ISV

This seems like a shocking solution: total annihilation. It's basically saying that, when Belial corrupts a place and a people, then nothing can be saved. It's ruined forever. Don't settle there, don't linger there. The implication is that you'll be fouled by a taint of evil that is virtually impossible to eradicate.

Belial turns up once again in Deuteronomy where the people are warned not to harden their hearts against their needy neighbours, just because a sabbatical year is approaching and debts will have to be cancelled. Then it turns up for a third and fourth time in a story of abuse and violence so repulsive that, down through the centuries of Israelite history, it was remembered as a generational source of depravity. It's in this story that, for the first time, we can link Belial to **abuse**, to **armies**, to **group mind control**, and to **perversion**.

This is the final story in the book of Judges: that of the Levite and his concubine. It's a story so revolting the compiler of the book was obviously reluctant to identify the Levite by name and ancestry. But at one point it becomes devastatingly clear this Levite was the grandson of Moses. And he was not the innocent victim he portrayed himself as being, when he rallied the tribes of Israel to go to war against the clan of Benjamin.

The Levite's name was Jonathan. This is not prince Jonathan, the friend of David—but a man who lived a few generations previously. To pick up his story half-way through, he'd gone down to Bethlehem to his father-in-law's house. His concubine—his second wife—had left him and gone home to her parents.

Red flag? Quite possibly. The only previous occasion where Scripture mentions a concubine running away, it was Hagar. Because of abuse. Consider too: there had to be an extremely good reason for the concubine's parents to accept her return against societal pressure.

Anyway, Jonathan arrived at Bethlehem to win her back. She agreed to go. Was some love-bombing involved? If so, it didn't last long. Together with a servant, they left on an eighty-kilometre journey late in the afternoon and made it as far as Gibeah of Benjamin by nightfall. They finally secured overnight lodging, only to be surrounded by some 'sons of Belial' who demanded the Levite come out so they could have sex with him. The host offered his daughter instead but, eventually, the concubine was thrust out the door. She was gang-raped and, at first light, as she lay dying, she reached out to touch the threshold. In doing so, she effectively accused her husband and the host of breaking covenant with her and of making her into a sacrifice to save themselves.

By the rites of hospitality that existed for centuries before that time and continue to the present day, when she passed over the threshold, the host became her covenant defender. He should have given his life to save her.

Everyone—Jonathan the Levite, the host, and the 'sons of Belial' in Gibeah—violated covenant in one way or another.

Now so far, we have a clear connection between sons of Belial and **abuse**. We're about to see **perversion, armies** and **group mind control**.

Jonathan decided on a gruesome act to gain the attention of the nation. He cut up his wife's body and sent the pieces around the twelve tribes as a call to war. It was an act of perversion—on two counts. The call to war was never meant to pit the entire tribal brotherhood against one clan, nor was a human body to be so defiled. He should have used a bullock. He should also have buried his wife and mourned her with honour before the day's end. He made every recipient of a piece of her cadaver unclean. The shock was so great they responded at once—heading off to find out what this terrible obscenity was all about.

Notice what happened? Jonathan spread **abuse** through the tribes. And in their shock, outrage and defilement, they didn't think entirely straight when his story was presented to them. The tribe of Benjamin in particular snapped into defence mode, deciding to protect the town of Gibeah along with the murderers and rapists it sheltered. They chose to go to war, rather than be the instruments of justice, and in doing so completely lost sight of how many additional innocent lives would be sacrificed in shielding the guilty.

Long story short: not only was the entire population of Gibeah wiped out, which was in keeping with the Deuteronomic Law about total destruction—but so was almost all the tribe of Benjamin, which was not. Just 600 men survived, a mere 2% of their pre-war numbers. No women or children were left. The armies of Israel were horrified—they'd meant to teach the tribe of Benjamin a lesson, not wipe them out.

Now at this point it's evident that **group mind control** was operating full-force. Because, having just wept with remorse over all this unnecessary killing, they immediately decided on some more. Realising that no men had responded to the call to war from Jabesh Gilead, they sent a troop to destroy the town and slaughter everyone there. Everyone, that is, except for 400 young virgins who were taken as trophies of war and given to the 600 survivors of the genocide in order to rebuild the tribe.

You might think the Israelites, having destroyed Gibeah, would fulfil the remainder of the Law by ensuring it was never rebuilt. But instead, a generation or so down the track, they went to the opposite extreme.

It was the first capital of the kingdom of all the tribes: Saul's designated royal seat.

It's not entirely clear in Scripture who the people in the recorded stories actually understood Belial to be. There is no explicit statement: 'Belial is the spirit of abuse.' Yet the common theme in the stories about the 'sons of Belial' is violent, abusive behaviour.

On the other hand, the writings from Second Temple period—which includes the time of Jesus and the early Christian era—are very clear regarding Belial. They are also clear about the origin of demons, a question that is never addressed in the Bible as we currently have it.

Michael Heiser comments that Belial was one of the names for the leader of the Watchers—the rebel angels who descended to Mount Hermon and there made a pact with each other to seek out human women and mate with them.[9] Another name was Samyaza,[10] yet another was Mastema and another was the Prince of Darkness.[11]

There were many variations on the Watcher story, but the most detailed comes from the Book of 1 Enoch. While this collection of writings is not part of the canon of Scripture in the west,[12] it was quoted and referenced in the epistle of Jude and is alluded to in Peter's letters. The Book of 1 Enoch was immensely popular in the first century and forms the background to Peter's discussion of the flood and the angels imprisoned in Tartarus, the netherhell.

According to 1 Enoch, the children fathered by Belial and his cohort were angel-human hybrids. Belial, along with the Watchers led by him, crossed both a spatial-boundary and a species-boundary to produce the *nephilim*—the giants of old. In addition, the Watchers passed forbidden knowledge to their wives and children: of particular concern were the arts of seduction, war and the occult. Enoch helps us make sense of Scripture's cryptic comment:

> *The nephilim were on the earth in those days—and also afterward—when the sons of God went to the daughters of humans and had children by them. They were the heroes of old, men of renown.*
>
> Genesis 6:4 NIV

The *nephilim*, the giants, were the children of angels. The mighty 'heroes of old', the *gibborim*, were the children of the *nephilim*. The Greek word often used for them was *titans*. Both the *nephilim* and the *gibborim* ravaged the earth to the point where the very existence of humanity was under threat. Their huge, voracious appetites, their rapacious consumption of resources, their vicious fighting and their continued interbreeding with humanity was devastating. Their activities brought the human species to the absolute brink of extinction.

Only at that point did God intervene. He had to. His promise to redeem humanity would never be able to be fulfilled if there were no genuine humans left.

So He sent the flood. The *nephilim* and *gibborim*—along with anyone not fully human—were destroyed in the deluge. At least, to be strictly accurate, their flesh was destroyed. Their spirits remained on the earth. Unlike human spirits, they are barred from heaven. And these spirits, still craving to be united with human flesh, became 'shedim', *demons*, or part of the realm of the 'rephaim', *ghosts*.

One question that baffles an extraordinary number of people is this: if the Watchers were imprisoned in the netherhell, and the *nephilim* and *gibborim* were 'unbodied', so to speak, in the flood, then where did giants like Goliath come from?

When the Israelites pass over from Egypt into their own inheritance in the Promised Land, they were given explicit instructions to totally annihilate some peoples but to deal diplomatically with others—and it becomes clear, on examination, that the difference lies in whether or not there are non-human bloodlines in the population. Yet Scripture does not record a second incursion of Watchers. So how did this happen? Did some *nephilim* survive the flood in fleshly form? Did the Watchers escape Tartarus for a time?

My personal opinion is that, no, the Watchers did not escape and, no, none of the *nephilim* survived and, no, there was not a second incursion either. I think Scripture alludes to what happened, when Moses gave his final speech:

> *Ask your parents or any of your elders. They will tell you that God Most High gave land to every nation. He assigned a guardian angel to each of them, but the Lord Himself takes care of Israel.*
>
> Deuteronomy 32:7–9 CEV

A more literal translation is:

> *When the Most High apportioned the nations, when He divided humankind, He fixed the boundaries of the peoples according to the number of the gods.*
>
> Deuteronomy 32:8 NRS

Basically this tells us *when* it happened—it happened when God divided humanity into different peoples: that coincides with the Tower of Babel. Later versions of the Hebrew text change the words, *'the number of the gods',* to *'the number of the sons of Israel'*. That sanitises the thought considerably but doesn't alter the actual number. It's seventy—the count of Jacob's descendants who go down to Egypt with him and also the count of the angels who were given different national territories to shepherd and steward.

These were not the same angels as the Watchers—instead these are the principalities. They were entrusted by God with guarding the peoples of the earth, except for those who were Jacob's descendants and who were to be the inheritors of the land promised to Abraham. Over time, these angels too fell. They became oppressors and perpetrated injustice. And they were worshipped as gods. I believe they are the source of the giants like Anak, Ahiman, Seshai and Talmai as well as Goliath and his brothers.

The post-Flood giants aren't, in my view, the result of an angelic insurrection against God like the one mounted by the Watchers. Rather, they came about because of a descent into corruption by God's appointed spiritual rulers. Perhaps it is not surprising that, when they fell, these seventy principalities set up their council headquarters in the very place the Watchers had come down—Mount Hermon.

The spirits of the dead *nephilim* and *gibborim* were understood, as previously mentioned, to be the *demons.* They were the 'shedim', mentioned in Deuteronomy 32:17 not long after the comment about apportioning the nations to the angels. Actually and more precisely, the 'shedim' are considered to be *goat demons.*[13]

I think that nuance is significant, because it's my personal opinion that the original sense of Belial was *goat lord.*[14] The name might indeed mean *worthless* or *nothing* but it's got a distinct resonance of *mountain goat* to it as well.[15]

Frequently titled 'the prince of demons', Belial is not a demon in his own right. Let's reiterate the distinction. A demon is the spirit of a dead—drowned—angel-human hybrid. Belial on the other hand is a fallen angel, a mighty general of infernal armies. A demon is a footsoldier in those armies—it's not a fallen angel, but the spirit of the deceased offspring of one.

Under the name Samyaza, Belial is the leader of the Watchers—a group of two hundred angels who, according to the Book of 1 Enoch, descended to Mount Hermon with the intention of seeking out human mates amongst the beautiful women of earth. This is not simply a case of angelic lust—at least lust for human women. It's actually lust for power; lust for destruction. It's an attempt to wreck God's plans for the redemption of humanity. The agenda is not so much the seduction of women as the ruination of God's promise in Eden, when He declares to the serpent:

> *I will put enmity between you and the woman, and between your seed and her seed. He will crush your head, and you will strike his heel.*
>
> Genesis 3:15 BSB

Here God pledges that the offspring of a woman will crush the offspring of the serpent. It's no coincidence the Watchers targeted the women when they could just have easily set their sights on the men—and corrupting them through access to power.

> *The sons of God saw the daughters of men they were were fair and they took ... wives.*
>
> Genesis 6:2 KJV

That word *fair* is 'tov'—the very same word God uses when He is pleased to describe His work of creation. It's *good. Excellent* of its kind. It's also *beautiful, agreeable, pleasant, sweet, kind, fruitful*. This doesn't say the women were perfect, but it does have the overtone that, basically, they were morally good—definitely *not* evil—as well as physically lovely.

David Flynn suggests that this verse might be better translated: *'The B'nai Elohim saw the daughters of Adam, that they were fit extensions.'* In other words, 'fit extensions'[16] indicates that the fallen angels saw an opening, a potential weakness, through which full-blown corruption could be introduced into the human genetic pattern, as well as into our spiritual and psychological makeup.

This wasn't a couple of hundred raunchy bad-boy angels just deciding to jump into bed with the hottest, sexiest women they could find on planet earth, this was a conspiracy to wipe out humanity and slap God down in the process. It was an attempt to make God's word null and void by making it impossible for a fully human Saviour to ever exist. It was betrayal of the most heinous kind.

It's a stratospheric leap from Adam's unplanned fall into sin to the dark and premeditated sedition of the Watchers. Adam and Eve weren't ever wandering around Eden, thinking, 'How can I betray God today?'[17] They fell into a trap. But the Watchers—at least those of their number who descended to Mount Hermon—were intent on treachery. They cooked up an invasion so malevolent that the trap set in Eden looks almost innocuous by comparison.[18]

The Book of Enoch says that, before the Watchers were confined, they came to the realisation that they'd made a massive mistake in begetting their monstrous offspring. Weeping, they asked Enoch to ascend to God and take Him a message, asking if they could return to heaven. Enoch did and received the answer. It was *no*.

And when we look at the story and see that it was more about high treason than lust for feminine flesh, we can see why there is no redemption for the fallen angels. The Watchers possessed a hatred of God so deep that they found it necessary to corrupt His image in His human children. It was not enough to exterminate those children; they had to be the agents of their own destruction. They were therefore shown how to forge weapons to wage war, how to use occult techniques of spell-casting and spell-binding, how to make poisons. Admittedly the skills the angels revealed also contained much useful and positive knowledge—but that's always the lure, isn't it?

So, allowing the angels who devised such atrocities back into the courts of heaven would have been extremely unwise. What accord, as Paul asked, has Christ with Belial? What concord can there be between the mind of God, set on returning humanity to Himself, and Belial, set on turning us against the Father? This is one of the most significant reversals Belial wants to set in motion: to brainwash children and turn them out to war against their parents—both human and divine—and likewise to cause parents to hate and battle their own children. This explains why I have often called Belial the 'Janissary spirit'.

A 'Janissary'[19] is a term coming from the Ottoman Empire and it originally referred to young Christian boys who were taken from their parents, inducted into the Sultan's army, brainwashed and converted, and then sent out to fight the Sultan's wars—including those conflicts that involved their own families. It was a cunning strategy: turn the sons against their fathers and get the enemy of the Empire to resource the war against themselves.[20]

Belial's agenda is not just to turn children against their fathers but to actually kill the parents. Failing that, the children are programmed to destroy their father's ideals and beliefs. This is true in both the natural and the spiritual. This tactic is a reversal of God the Son taking sin on Himself.

Worse still, we are a source of mockery for those who have deceived us so successfully we fund the very systems set up to exterminate us.[21] Belial has been remarkably successful in this endeavour over the last few decades and, through mind control, has hidden its gameplan all too well. It's thus all too easy to see Belial as the cause of sin in the world, but that's not so. Like other threshold spirits, it sets up various tests, but we make the choices. Demons and fallen cosmic powers are catalysts for those choices, but they are not the cause of them—even when they prompt us to destroy ourselves.

Ultimately Belial's target is fathers and fatherhood and, most especially of all, our heavenly Father. However, it always attacks the mother first—or else waits until the mother is out of the way. Armies, by design, lack any of the gentler aspects of kindness and nurture to do with motherhood but that's not the main arena where this spirit deploys this policy. Paedophiles are opportunistic in targeting—in particular—young boys just after they've lost their mother. Dad is usually not coping at that point and he's immensely grateful for a father figure stepping in to help his son through the emotional crisis while he is struggling with his own grief around death or divorce. He's blinded to the grooming of his son and, in not noticing, he's often the one the son blames most in later life: 'Dad didn't defend me when I needed him most.'

This is so common that, as the church, we need to be more pro-active in watching out for it. We need to be 'Watchers' of a new kind. Because instead of protecting children, most churches have protected the abusers and re-traumatised the abused. In fact, as a whole, the church has created a haven for abusers. Perversely the very institution meant to be a sanctuary for the wounded, binding up the broken-hearted, has become a refuge for exploiters.

I believe the reason the spirit of abuse makes its move when the woman is out of the picture is because the greatest danger to its ultimate success is not the father but the mother. God made the promise of a redeemer who would crush the serpent's head to Eve, not to Adam. That's what fuels Belial's relentless hatred of women.

In our present era, the war on mothers and motherhood, women and girls is disguised under a cloak of 'inclusivity'. The various attempts to erase women, cancel mothers and eradicate girls simply demonstrate Belial's loathing of the gender. Men are not safe—they are in fact the real target, and will not save themselves by hiding in the shadows during the ideological war. Because exactly as in a game of chess, while the greatest threat is the queen, the objective is to take out the king.

That's always been Belial's playbook. And a page from it was used in the Garden of Eden. The regent Adam was the primary target, but his battle companion and helper Eve had to be taken out first.

With the 'Janissary' aspect as a significant face of Belial, we see once again the full-force tactics of **abuse, group mind control, armies** and **inversions**, but we should now include in the list of its activities three of its more insidious strategies:

- grooming of the sons in order to **turn them against their fathers**
- deceiving believers into **resourcing the war against themselves**
- convincing believers to **fund the very systems that will destroy them.**

Those elements—the turning of the sons against the fathers, and the resourcing of the enemy in their war against ourselves—also appear in the story of the Watchers. The fallen angels not only betrayed the Father of all creation, they influenced humanity to side with them. By teaching men and women how to make weapons for war and instructing them in magic—which is simply the use of the creative power of God against

Him—the Watchers set humanity on a path towards self-destruction. People therefore resourced the war against themselves. The depravity became so bad:

> *The Lord observed the extent of human wickedness on the earth, and He saw that everything they thought or imagined was consistently and totally evil.*
>
> Genesis 6:5 NLT

Instead of permitting the Watchers to return, as they'd begged, God sent the flood to destroy and cleanse everything they'd tainted—and imprisoned the Watchers in the netherhell of Tartarus. It may seem a harsh, unyielding judgment but, consider: these Watchers were apparently throne guardians. Their Aramaic name means *the wakeful ones, the never-sleeping ones*, suggesting they were the many-eyed cherubim and thus heavenly sons who were always permitted in His presence. They were the closest to God, aware of His plans, belonging to His court—essentially His confidants. They weren't low-ranking angels who carried messages; they were part of the governmental structure of heaven—the Divine Council.[22] They were top of the hierarchy and, while they obviously didn't know the fine detail of everything, they knew sufficient to be able to sabotage the work of redemption. The level of betrayal is unimaginable—they not only cursed each other and took an oath to complete their treachery, they were, in effect, cursing God's love and mercy. They blighted His compassion and then expected to be able to access it anyway.

Now not all Watchers joined the conspiracy, but enough of them did to wreak havoc on earth. And they came within a whisker of success. Only one family stood between them and total triumph. Now we may not be able to be sure of the veracity of all the small details in the Book of Enoch but, from Peter's writings, we can be sure of this—the Watchers were definitely imprisoned in Tartarus and the flood was sent to purify the earth.

It's crucial to recognise that Belial's temptations always involve transgression across forbidden boundaries. Just as the angels left their appointed estate and crossed a line never meant to be crossed, so Belial tries to entice us over thresholds into prohibited territory. Jude, in his epistle, mentions the transgressions of these rebel angels, only to move straight on to speaking about the inhabitants of Sodom and Gomorrah. The similarity of the incident involving the Levite and his concubine at Gibeah to Lot's behaviour at Sodom begs the question as to whether the men of Sodom were 'sons of Belial'.

While there is no explicit statement to that effect, perhaps there are clues in the names. One possible meaning of Sodom is *demons*,[23] thus making a connection between Sodom in the Valley of Siddim to 'shedim', *the goat demons*. In a later age, half a millennia into the future, the Valley of Siddim was the Valley of Shittim, *acacias*, where the Israelites encamped on their last stop before crossing the Jordan.[24] The defilement on the landscape was still so great that the people should have remembered God's prohibition on such places:

> *Burn the town... It will remain a permanent mound of ruins, never to be rebuilt again.*
>
> Deuteronomy 13:16 ISV

They should have taken the hint encoded in the word *acacia*. In Hebrew, it has the sense *turn aside*. It was in the Valley of Acacias that the people began to worship Baal Peor, *the lord of the opening*. Through ritual sex and eating food offered to idols, the Israelites covenanted with an obvious threshold guardian—indicated by both the name, *lord of the opening*, and the fact they were, at long last, on the threshold of the Promised Land after forty years of wandering. Their betrayal of God meant they lost His covering protection and, when they were visited by a plague that killed 24,000 people, they had to rely on the defence of Baal Peor, the spirit with whom they had forged their agreement.

This episode highlights the centuries-long contamination of the landscape around Sodom. The Valley of Siddim was a spiritual dead zone—ground zero for spiritual radiation so deadly and so potent it can never be eradicated.

Except... there is a hint of hope in a couplet of miracles Jesus performed.[25]

But first, we have stop being complicit with the enemy. We have to stop handing over to our spiritual opponents the resources to destroy us. We have to seek to uncover our own transgressions by asking God to remove the veil of mind control blinding us to the reality that we are much more comfortable in the camp of Kronos or Belial than we are with Jesus of Nazareth.

When I first noticed mind control as a tactic of Belial and started to pray about it, I focused on other people. I added myself in as an afterthought, not because I believed I was genuinely affected, but because I didn't want to create an 'us vs. them' mentality. However, after a month of prayer, I started to see my behaviour differently. I began to realise that those people I would have classed as champions of the abused had, in fact, slipped into abuse themselves—and, in siding with them, I was effectively allying myself with the enemy of our souls.

Because the spirit of abuse is a threshold guardian, it will test us at different times.

- first, on the threshold into our calling;
- second, when we happen to be working with someone who is on the threshold of their own calling;
- third, whenever we move into a significant new aspect of our divine vocation.

Just look at the tests Jesus faced as He was about to take up His ministry.

Prayer

Lord, I feel helpless. And sometimes helplessness overwhelms me like a flood.

Lord, I feel hopeless. And sometimes hopelessness shakes my soul like an earthquake.

I look up to You and, instead of sensing Your comfort, I feel like the sky is falling in. I panic and procrastinate and then, when I run out of time, I spiral into more helplessness and hopelessness.

Sometimes I put my hope in Time. But sometimes I sense in my spirit the danger of doing that, and instead I put my trust in the guardians of Time, those legendary beings with one-hundred hands. And then I feel pulled one hundred ways and I don't know what to do.

Heavenly Father, I don't know how many covenants my ancestors have raised with different entities of the spirit world. And I don't know the ways in which I have tacitly agreed to them throughout my life. I do know that, although my mind tells me I don't believe in Time as a healer or Time being on my side, my heart has a secret longing for that to be true. My heart hides itself even from me—but it does not hide from You. So search me, Lord, and bring to light the concealed beliefs that keep me from all-out surrender to You.

I repent of my false refuges and I name them before You …

I repent also of the specific false refuge of putting my faith in the thought the suffering would end and my agreement to the lie it might never end.

I ask Jesus of Nazareth to empower my words of confession and repentance, so that I truly will turn away from those habits of comfort that substitute for You as my refuge in times of trouble.

I ask You, in Your own perfect timing, to annul any covenant with Time, with Death or with Hell in my family line and in my life. I ask Jesus to bring the eternal NOW of His presence to dwell with us. I ask Him, in His perfect timing, to redeem the time I have wasted and to take me into that covenantal space that is raised in time but is beyond time.

I'm so sorry I put my trust in the passing of Time instead of You. I'm so sorry I agreed to the pass over of Time into my life, instead of relying on You. Please evict Time and its agents, allies, associates and guardians from my life. I invite Your Holy Spirit to dwell in me and I accept Your invitation to dwell in You.

Forgive me for my complicity with Time, the child-destroyer. I thought I was fighting the spirit of abuse when, in reality, I've had an alliance with it. I ask Immanuel to grant me the eternal NOW of His presence and I ask Him to help me to always call on Him—so my hope is in Him, not in the power of Time itself to ease my wounds.

I ask the Holy Spirit, having evicted the spirits of abuse and time in my life, to seal closed any access doors to these unholy ones and to keep me and hide me in the timeless covenant of the blood of Jesus.

In His name, the name of Jesus of Nazareth, Yeshua HaMashiach, Immanuel. Amen.

4
Tests and Tabernacles

THERE ARE MANY DIFFERENT WAYS to examine the temptations Jesus faced, but I want to look at them in the light of what Jude, the servant of Jesus and the brother of James, says about transgressions across forbidden boundaries. Jude pulls absolutely no punches, shattering the 'gentle Jesus' image with a stark reminder:

> *For certain men have crept in among you unnoticed—ungodly ones who were designated long ago for condemnation. They turn the grace of our God into a license for immorality, and they deny our only Master and Lord, Jesus Christ.*
>
> *Although you are fully aware of this, I want to remind you that after Jesus had delivered His people out of the land of Egypt, He destroyed those who did not believe.*
>
> *And the angels who did not stay within their own domain but abandoned their proper dwelling— these He has kept in eternal chains under darkness, bound for judgment on that great*

> *day. In like manner, Sodom and Gomorrah and the cities around them, who indulged in sexual immorality and pursued strange flesh, are on display as an example of those who sustain the punishment of eternal fire.*
>
> Jude 1:4–7 BSB

'He destroyed those who did not believe': not something we like to recall. There was the plague that struck the people because of the golden calf,[26] the deaths from snakebite when the people grumbled, the followers of Korah, Dathan and Abiram who were swallowed by the earth for questioning God's decrees—and so many more. Many people put these incidents in a mental box labelled 'vengeful God of the Old Testament', close and lock it while comforting themselves with the thought that Jesus is about love and grace.

Jude smashes this illusion. That Destroyer was Jesus, he says.

Our failure to understand threshold covenant means we don't comprehend the gravity of the promises made by the Israelites. But they knew what they were agreeing to: they wanted the blessings and were willing to risk the curses.

The first Passover occurred while the Israelites were still in Egypt: it was a threshold covenant. The blood on the lintels and doorposts wasn't something novel or new. It was a completely ordinary, everyday sign repurposed from longstanding rites of hospitality. It was the standard display by a householder painted at a doorway as a welcome to an honoured guest. It carried with it an invitation to covenant, to partnership and to mutual defence. That was the incentive to participate in the first Passover: divine defence.

To accept the covenant, all that was necessary was to pass over the blood pooled in the cornerstone under the lintel. To refuse the covenant, a person would strike the cornerstone or dash their foot against it.

A threshold covenant is *not* the same as a blood covenant, though both involve sacrifice. They, in turn, are both different to name covenants—which, generally speaking, do not involve blood. In terms of divine covenants—that is, covenants between humanity and God—it's worth spelling out the significant differences. These differences are not necessarily the same as those in covenants between human beings, nor of course between humans and other spiritual beings.

Blood covenant: one-sided in both blessing and cursing. Like Abram, asleep when God cut a covenant with him, we are asleep—dead in our sins—when God raises a blood covenant with us. It's all His doing and all His responsibility. Through a blood covenant, we come into the family of God. Our status moves from **creature** to **child**.

Name covenant: two-sided. We're now awake and able to take responsibility for accepting or rejecting the offer of a new—or renewed—name. A name exchange is involved—God will reveal a hidden name for Himself and will announce a new name for us, as He did when He told Abram His name was 'El Shaddai' and called him 'Abraham'. Our status is enhanced to friendship: we become both **child** and **companion**. Now there is the possibility of something previously inconceivable: betrayal. Enemies, by their very nature, cannot betray one another. Betrayal is only possible for friends.[27]

Threshold covenant: two-sided. If we accept the new name God offers, we also agree to a threshold covenant. We become responsible for our part in a relationship of mutual defence, we sign on the dotted line, so to speak, regarding a partnership with God. Our status is again enhanced: **child, companion** and now **colleague** as well. But with the summons across the divine cornerstone onto heaven's sapphire floor to take up our calling, we are about to face interviews, confrontations and tests that will reveal the true state of our heart. Basically we've been presented with an opportunity to join God's staff team and He allows the council of heaven to be in on the selection process.

It's not about whether or not we'll ever make a mistake in relation to our calling. Mistakes are going to happen. But unintentional error is not betrayal. If we get as close to God as His throne guardians—and God will allow us to do so—will we betray Him like the Watchers who descended to Mount Hermon? Can we be tempted over the boundaries that are never meant to be crossed?

Jude's epistle recalls three instances where thresholds were crossed, and disasters occurred. The first is when Jesus brought the people out of Egypt but, through their betrayal of the covenant of mutual defence they'd initiated, they were destroyed before they could reach their inheritance. The second instance is that of the angels who left their appointed places to mate with human women. The third instance is that of Sodom and Gomorrah—intriguingly, Jude hints that the men of Sodom were aware Lot's visitors were angels.

Jude points out that the temptation might be severe, but the consequences are so dire they are unthinkable. Two of his three examples involve Belial. Quite possibly the third—the reason for the destruction of the people of Israel in the desert—does too.

In *Dealing with Python*, I looked at Python's involvement in the temptation of Jesus in the wilderness as He approached the threshold of His public ministry. Now I want to examine how Belial contributed to the gameplay. Jesus had been fasting for forty days when the satan appeared and said: 'If You are the Son of God, tell this stone to become bread.'[28]

Jesus had obviously reached the stage where His body desperately needed sustenance. And at that point, the satan introduced a boundary-crossing temptation. It wasn't as much about satisfying hunger as it was about different 'kinds'. Bread and stones are of a different 'kind'. Just as angels and humans are of a different 'kind'. When God created creatures after their own kinds,[29] He meant for there to be proper boundaries between the different species.

To break down those barriers is to create unknown perils. Angel-human hybrids were giants whose spirits are demons.

When the satan tempted Jesus, the test he presented was really a choice between magic and miracle. Multiplying bread from bread is a miracle that does not transgress 'kinds' and is in keeping with God's work of multiplying grain from a single seed sown in the ground into a head of wheat. However, the satan wanted Jesus to change the essential 'kind' of a stone, to tell it to change the assigned boundaries of its nature: to use the creative power of the Word to disrupt the limitations God had built into the universe from the very start.

Let me repeat the simplest definition of magic: using the creative power of God against Him.

Yet there was more than that to the test. Deeper than a temptation to assuage His hunger through magic, Jesus was being asked to align Himself with the fallen Watchers through the same kind of sin. It might not have been sexual in nature, but it involved the same boundary-crossing of 'kinds' that Jude warned so bluntly about.

Until the twentieth century, the deeper nuances of this temptation weren't particularly relevant to us. But now science has discovered how to tamper with 'kinds' in order to alter species—introducing, for example, parts of fish DNA into potatoes so that insects will leave them alone. And that's the least of it.

God does not ban breeding the same kinds together—only transgressing boundaries. Our world routinely tampers with genetic material while believers think Scripture has nothing to say on the matter. But Jesus drew a line in the sand for us. We ignore that line at a stupendous cost.

And that's so easy to do. Group mind control is pervasive across the entire globe.

I have considerable doubts the fallen Watchers intended to create monsters. I'm sure they theorised they could beget offspring who would be much, much better than the 'good' that Yahweh had brought forth. More beautiful, more intelligent, more talented, more excellent in every way.

Like the hubris of these angels is the hubris of so much modern science: the belief that our partly-tested theories must be right. Whether this concerns mRNA technology or sub-atomic particles, we've been bombarded with the mantra 'the science is settled'.

When I was teaching science last century, my first words to a new class on the first day of their first semester were always: 'Two-thirds of what I am about to teach you this year is rubbish. Never forget that. The problem is that no one will know which two-thirds until about a century from now.'

The history of science is littered with faulty ideas that seemed flawless. The science is never settled. The faith in theory that has become the bedrock belief of so many modern scientists would be commendable if it weren't such a tragic sell-out of the very fundamentals of the discipline. Untested theory isn't science. It hardly even qualifies as religion, since most religious people put their faith to the test at some point. They want positive results when they pray.

Science used to be built on the premise of making a hypothesis and testing that hypothesis repeatedly in experiments until consistent, reproducible results were obtained. 'Science' is now simply a convenient invocation in certain settings, and terribly inconvenient in others. As we stare down the barrel of transhumanism and eugenics into a pit of total unknowns, we keep being reassured by those who have no skin in the game that it's perfectly safe.

Just as Jesus was informed by the satan it was perfectly safe to throw Himself down from the pinnacle of the Temple.

Having refused to turn stones into bread, the devil tried again. Whether the satan—which is simply a title meaning *the adversary*—was the same spirit in subsequent tests as in the first one is unknown. The general unquestioned assumption is: yes, it is. However, in the time of Jesus there was thought to be multiple satans.

So the threshold spirits might have lined up for the opportunity to test Jesus but, more likely, they conspired together as a cabal of plotters. The spirit of Python was undoubtedly there, evidenced by the very wording of the temptations. Belial, too, has to have been part of the collusion because of the boundary-transgression aspects. After all, the test wasn't about obedience to the Torah, like, 'Oh look, roast pork on a campfire! Go for it, Jesus.' There was nothing in the Law to say *don't turn rocks into bread*. Instead it was much more profound—a quantum level of disobedience over and above consuming pig.

The satan, whoever it was, basically responds to Jesus with the following: 'Think I'm worried about Scriptural verses? I'll take Your Deuteronomy 8:3, *"Man shall not live on bread alone, but on every word that comes from the mouth of God"* and raise You a small sampling from Psalm 91, *"He will command His angels concerning You to guard You in all Your ways. They will lift You up in their hands, so that You will not strike Your foot against a stone."'*

This really did raise the stakes—and in more than one way. In the time of Jesus, Psalm 91 was seen as a protective talisman against the powers of evil. Actually, I've known believers who recite it daily nowadays with a similar attitude.

The satan just laughed. By quoting the psalm, he was indicating he was completely unperturbed by it. It wouldn't concern him for anyone to use it against him;

he could airily say it himself. However, there was an inbuilt trick in this test. Part of the calling of Jesus was to be a rabbi, a teacher. And by quoting a psalm, the satan challenged that aspect of Jesus' calling by using a very fine example of traditional rabbinic technique. It was such a subtle double-bind, it was no longer a matter of just saying 'no' to the devil; a lot depended on *how* Jesus said 'no'.

This is the same kind of manipulative technique used by the leader who, when I took a problem to him about a communication issue, said, 'I thought you knew me better than that. Do you really think that of me?' It's designed as a double-bind; whether you say *yes* or *no*, you're in trouble.

If Jesus had come back with the next verse from Psalm 91 or a defence based on it, He was accepting the devil's implied offer. 'I'll be Your rabbi, Your mentor, Your counsellor, Your teacher': that's what the satan was declaring and proposing. It didn't really matter if Jesus jumped from the pinnacle of the Temple or not if He came back with any part of Psalm 91.

However, He responded with: *'Do not put the Lord your God to the test,'* from Deuteronomy 6:16. It's important to note that Jesus made a selection here. The full verse is: *'Do not test the Lord your God as you tested Him at Massah.'* There are in fact times when God invites us to test Him.

There's the well-known verse from Malachi, where God says to His people, *'Test Me in this.'* [30] And there's the prophet Isaiah who, after God had spoken to King Ahaz, telling him to ask for a sign, seriously rebuked the king for what seemed like a pious response: *'I will not put the Lord to the test.'*[31]

So clearly it's not simply a matter of quoting Scripture so the devil will flee. Some people think that, if we know Scripture well enough, spiritual warfare will mean dipping into the arsenal for the nearest weapon. But, as Jesus shows, we have to be in relationship with the Father and so deeply dependent on the Holy Spirit that we know *which* verse to apply *when*.

This second temptation also has other profound aspects that have a great deal of bearing on what prerequisites we need to have in place before we can successfully confront Belial. There are **timing** aspects to this test, as well as **cornerstone** aspects.

These aspects are not at all obvious without considerable background information. There are two kinds of time in the spiritual realm: ordinary time and appointed time. In Greek, *ordinary* time is 'chronos' and *appointed time* is 'kairos'. In Hebrew, the word for *appointed time* is 'moed'. Other words for time, 'eth' and 'iddan', are related to *testimony*.[32]

The feast days, the fast days and the festivals of Israel were—with a few exceptions—divinely *appointed times*.

These include, importantly for the purposes of this book, Yom Kippur, *the Day of Atonement*, and Sukkot, *the Feast of Tabernacles*. There was a forty-day period, ending on Yom Kippur, that was considered a traditional time of repentance and fasting but nevertheless was not mandated by God. It commemorated the time that Moses had spent on Mount Sinai repenting before God for the sin of the golden calf and receiving the second set of tablets engraved with the Ten Commandments.

There are faint clues in the gospels that Jesus was baptised at the very beginning of this forty-day period, on the first day of the month of Elul, and was then driven by the Holy Spirit into the wilderness where He stayed until He was tempted on the tenth day of Tishrei, Yom Kippur.[33] Coming out of the desert the following day, He was identified by John the Baptist back at Bethany-beyond-the-Jordan, was then followed by five disciples to Galilee where He performed His first miracle at the wedding feast in Cana during the Festival of Sukkot. A pleasing line-up of appointed times there.

The significance of the Day of Atonement as the hour of Jesus' temptation should not be underestimated. It puts a whole new spin on the devil's agenda. I think it's possible to actually pinpoint the exact minute of this temptation. For a start, Jesus was out in the wilderness—driven out, just like the scapegoat would be on this most solemn of days—when the devil whisked Him to the very top of the Temple. After this nifty bit of translocation, the devil makes his challenge:

'If You are the Son of God... throw yourself down.
For it is written:
He will command His angels concerning You,
and they will lift You up in their hands,
so that You will not strike your foot against a stone.'

Matthew 4:6 BSB

Now what timing had the devil chosen? Well, if you wanted complete and total ruination, you'd pick the most critical moment to do it. You'd pick the moment when the high priest had just entered the Holy of Holies to sprinkle blood on the mercy-seat covering the Ark of the Covenant. You'd pick the moment when someone leaping across—*passing over*—the mercy-seat, the 'kapporeth' or *place of atonement*, would wreck that act of petition to God for the purification of the nation. Had Jesus actually jumped, He would have *passed over* the earthly counterpart of the cornerstone of the entire universe. And, because it was the satan who was the host—think about all that implies for a moment!—then by asking Jesus to step over the blood-stained cornerstone into his 'house', a threshold covenant would have been enacted.

When Adam was tempted and lured into acquiescing with the serpent, he lost his regency of the world. It passed into the possession of the prince of the power of the air, the spirit who rules the sons of disobedience. Had Christ actually jumped—and there is no question He would have been genuinely tempted to, otherwise there was no point to the test—He would have handed over the entire cosmos to the enemy. The first Adam succumbed and lost the earth; the second Adam would have, had He succumbed, lost the heavens as well.

The satan's ambition hadn't changed. He still wanted the throne of God. And getting Jesus to jump would have given it to him.

What did Kronos want at that very particular moment on the Day of Atonement? **To mess with the cornerstone.**

This is so important, I'm going to put it at the top of the list of its tactics—because it's not just about the cornerstone in the Temple at Jerusalem but also about the cornerstone of our lives. And as promised, I'm going to repeat that list. So far we have:

- **messing with the cornerstone**
- **group mind control**
- **double-bind manipulation**
- **inversion or perversion of symbols**
- **reversing victim and perpetrator**
- **complicity with the abusers by insisting on grace for them at the expense of the victims**
- **blame-shifting and defaming**
- **gaslighting or denying in such a way that both victims and observers question their perception of reality**
- **army mentality that darkens children's minds so that they see their parents as the enemy**

- **persuading us to resource the war against ourselves by arming and financing our enemies**
- **transgression of forbidden boundaries**
- **time-wasting or reliance on time passing**

There's one more. And it's yet another tactical stratagem by the spirit of abuse that's almost universally overlooked: **faking the covering cloud of glory**.

And that's the essence of the third test Jesus faced.

On the face of it, the third temptation simply involves naked power and raw ambition. Surely the devil knew Jesus better than that! I think it's highly likely it was actually an appeal to His pity, compassion and mercy. Perhaps even to goodness, kindness and faithfulness—the very Fruit of the Spirit that will overcome the spirit of abuse.

The devil deployed another teleportation and whizzed Jesus from the pinnacle of the Temple to a high mountain in order to show Him all the kingdoms of this world. It's not hard to deduce what mountain this was: it had to have been the highest one in Israel—snow-covered Mount Hermon, on the far northern border. Where else would the devil have all the kingdoms available to show?

This mountain was the landing zone of the fallen Watchers. More than that, it was also the place where, in Canaanite religion, Baal and his brothers, the seventy 'young lions', the godlings who were said to be the sons of Asherah, had their palaces. They were equivalent to the seventy angel-shepherds appointed by God to rule the nations after the rebellion at the Tower of Babel. Mount Hermon was the assembly point for these seventy principalities charged with the government of this world. It was their council headquarters.

Again Jesus must have found the temptation incredibly enticing. It had to be real to have any meaning, so I don't think this was an easy choice. The offer was so, so very close to His calling—and to bloodlessly depose Baal the so-called cloud-rider and claim that title for Himself would have been very difficult to turn down. Instead of a terrible and bloody war in the spirit realm that spilled over to untold violence on the earth, there could have been a calm, orderly transition. Jesus could have ushered in a rule of peace and plenty over the entire world. He could have fulfilled the prophecy of Psalm 82 and pronounced judgment on the principalities who ruled the nations then and there. He could have swept them aside, exchanging their corruption and cruelty for justice and mercy. The countless urgent prayers of people across the ages desperate for help now, *now, please please now*, would have burdened His heart. But His reign would have come at a tremendous cost—the loss of redemption for humanity. And, quite apart from anything else, the timing was wrong. It was two years and six days too early.

Again, we can be very precise in evaluating the timing. Two years and six days later,[34] Jesus returned to Mount Hermon. He was back and He'd come on His own terms. He'd just set the Cornerstone of the church in place and He was now almost ready to wrest power from the principalities of the nations. He only needed the tabernacling cloud of Yahweh as His covering. And that came down as He was transfigured in glory.

On the Day of Atonement in the year before Jesus died, He took His disciples to Caesarea Philippi, to the shrine of the goat-demon Pan. In going out to the wilderness and timing His visit to the infamous Gates of Hell in this way, He imaged Himself as the scapegoat sent to Azazel—another of the leaders amongst the fallen Watchers. There He asked His disciples who people thought He was. When Simon announced His own view that Jesus was the Messiah, Jesus said:

> *'I tell you that you are Peter, and on this rock I will build My church, and the gates of Hades will not overcome it. I will give you the keys of the kingdom of heaven; whatever you bind on earth will be bound in heaven, and whatever you loose on earth will be loosed in heaven.'*
>
> Matthew 16:18–19 NIV

This is a name covenant.[35] It involves a name exchange. We know that the name Simon received was, in Aramaic, 'Cephas'. That name is immensely significant. It isn't simply *rock*, it's a *cornerstone*. It's basically the same name as the ruling high priest, Caiaphas. It's about *atonement*, being related to the word 'kippur', in Yom Kippur, Day of Atonement, and also to 'kapporeth', *covering*, being the name for the *mercy seat* where the blood of atonement was sprinkled on this solemn day.

Jesus was replacing the government of the Jewish nation. He was emplacing a new cornerstone, establishing a covenant at the same time, and making His first governmental decree. His language is that of taking up authority: 'keys of the kingdom' refers to the right to open and close gates and thresholds, while 'binding' and 'loosing' refers to taking out a legal injunction.

On the Feast of Tabernacles, Jesus took His newly formed cabinet straight into enemy territory and declared war.

> *After six days Jesus took with Him Peter, James and John the brother of James, and led them up a high mountain by themselves. There He was transfigured before them. His face shone like the sun, and His clothes became as white as the light. Just then there appeared before them Moses and Elijah, talking with Jesus.*
>
> *Peter said to Jesus, 'Lord, it is good for us to be here. If You wish, I will put up three shelters—one for You, one for Moses and one for Elijah.'*
>
> *While he was still speaking, a bright cloud covered them, and a Voice from the cloud said,*

'This is My Son, whom I love; with Him I am well pleased. Listen to Him!'

Matthew 17:1–5 NIV

Jesus walked straight into Belial's territory, the mountain the devil had claimed for his own. Just over two years previously, Jesus had received an offer of worldwide dominion on this very spot. So His return basically said, 'I'm back. And I'm taking over. Your time is done. You had your chance. The war begins now.'

He was fulfilling the prophecy of Psalm 82. It's short and so mind-blowing that many translations try to pull back on the knock-out punch of the first verse.

> *God stands in the divine assembly; He judges among the gods...*
> *How long will you judge unjustly and show partiality to the wicked? Selah.*
> *Vindicate the weak and fatherless; do justice and maintain the rights of the afflicted and destitute.*
> *Rescue the weak and needy; rescue them from the hand of the wicked.*
> *The rulers do not know nor do they understand; they walk on in the darkness...*
> *All the foundations of the earth... are shaken.*
> *I said, 'You are gods; Indeed, all of you are sons of the Most High. Nevertheless you will die like men and fall like any one of the princes.'*
> *Arise, O God, judge the earth! For to You belong all the nations.*

Psalm 82:1–8 AMP

The concept of 'monotheism'—the belief that there is only one deity—is relatively modern. The Bible does not teach it. Nor is there an evolution of understanding in its pages going from a primitive belief in a pantheon of many godlings and goddesses towards a more sophisticated view that there is just one all-knowing, all-powerful Creator. Modern monotheism is one reason Belial is translated *worthless* and not given the status of a supernatural traitor.

The Bible however consistently teaches that, in a plurality of divine beings, Yahweh is unique. He alone created them—and us. He resides with them in the heavens. The Hebrew word 'elohim', sometimes translated *God* and at other times *gods* is, according to Michael Heiser, better rendered as *inhabitant of the heavenly realms*. This naturally includes God but is not limited to God. Everything depends on the context. As Heiser points out, modern monotheism reduces the Scriptural saying, *'There is no one like You amongst the gods'* to ironic mockery, *'There's no one like You amongst non-existent supernatural beings.'*

Yet this statement is about God as incomparable, one-of-a-kind, above and beyond the created order—not about only one supernatural being in the heavenlies.

Yahweh has a Divine Council, or Divine Assembly, mentioned many times in Scripture where He receives reports and renders judgment, where true prophets stand to hear His decrees, where He consults with His creation (yes, you can indeed raise your eyebrows!), where He sends out Watchers (yes, there's some good ones left) to announce the verdicts of the Council, where He deploys angelic agents (even some highly dubious ones) to bring those verdicts to fruition.

This Divine Council was mimicked by the fallen principalities on their Mount of Assembly. Jesus went up that very mountain with three of His disciples, up past the various shrines to the gods of the nations. He would have gone to the summit, to the highest temple of the ancient world. He would have passed through that temple and entered a spiral-walled sanctuary enclosing the mountaintop and leading to a bowl carved into it. He would have passed a limestone stele inscribed with the words: *'According to the command of the great bull god… those swearing an oath in this place, go forth.'* [36]

The President and Vice President of the United States do not travel together for security reasons. It's unimaginable that either of them would go to a hostile country to declare war, let alone together as a pair. Jesus obviously didn't get the memo on the dangers of such an operational procedure because He not only travelled with His clueless second-in-command and naïve lieutenants through spiritually hostile territory, He took them with Him when He strode straight to the heart of enemy headquarters on this planet, interrupted the war council of the assembled principalities, and told them all the authority delegated to them by God was withdrawn because of their acts of injustice and degeneracy. And He introduced them to the leading councillors of His new government.

That's what it means for Jesus to fulfil Psalm 82 in the way He did. His Transfiguration wasn't just a manifestation of glory; behind it was an immense weight of prophecy. There was no other place He could have done it on earth: it had to be on Hermon, the Mount of Assembly, the counterfeit of Zion, the precinct where the Canaanite godlings had their palaces, where the seventy 'young lions' were resident; the very same summit where so long ago the Watchers had descended and taken their oaths to mate with human women.

It is not obvious in the English translation of Psalm 82 that Jesus interrupts a strategy meeting, but the Hebrew word for *among* also has a nuance of *approach, battle* or *war*. So let me suggest for the first line: *'God stands up in the War Council of El, judging the gods.'*

Just as 'elohim' can mean *God* or *gods*, and is totally dependent on context, I strongly suspect that 'El' is just as ambiguous. Sometimes it means *God*, as in Yahweh, and sometimes it means *El*, as in the bull-god of the Canaanites.[37]

Mount Hermon, amongst all of its other religious associations, was also the site of the threshing floor of El, the bull-god. And a threshing floor was not just high ground to catch the wind in order to winnow grain that had been sledged, flailed or trodden on the floor, it also had other notable functions, including:

- communal assembly
- deliverance of judgment

- divination to seek divine insight
- portal between earth and heaven

The gospel accounts are so understated it's easy to miss how daring, courageous and audacious this action by Jesus was. In ascending Mount Hermon, He was enacting a government takeover. It wasn't the first time His actions were revolutionary. When He walked on water, He was exploding the claims of the goddess Asherah to the title, 'She Who Walks on Water'. When He multiplied the loaves and fishes, and called Himself the 'Bread of Heaven', He was reclaiming a title from the harvest godling Tammuz. When He gave sight to a man born blind and called Himself the 'Light of the World', He was telling the world that Mithras, the Persian godling of friendship who was the favourite of the occupying Roman forces, was an imposter who had usurped that title.

Jesus was constantly at war with the principalities of the nations—His seven 'I AM' statements recorded in John's gospel are claims to titles that, on the surface, belong to the first or principal deity of different Gentile nations. Through His miracles, He demonstrates His right to claim those titles back. But He didn't restrict Himself to miracles: His claim to be the Son of Man who would come on the clouds of heaven was the clinching factor that decided the outcome of His trial before Caiaphas.

He was claiming to be equal with Yahweh, and at the same time claiming that Baal the Cloud-Rider had stolen His identity.

The Cloud is a vital aspect of the confrontation on Mount Hermon. It was the covering that kept Him and His dim-witted apostles with Him safe in enemy territory. Jesus chose the day of His stand very carefully and deliberately. It was no coincidence that this was the Festival of Tabernacles—one of the appointed feasts of God. The *kairos* timing was exquisite.

Prayer

Heavenly Lord and gracious Father,

Our culture today specialises in tempting us into making a transgression of 'kinds'. From genetic manipulation of food and drugs, medical procedures and immunisation therapies, to declassification of gender, to words inverted in meaning, we're being subjected to constant gaslighting by political agencies, government bureaucracies and scientific authorities. In so many instances, we simply don't know what to believe.

We try to make Time work on our behalf by withdrawing to 'wait and see', but we're bullied and harassed by people who don't keep their own rules, and governments that break their own laws.

So, Lord, we just have to admit that it's almost certain we have transgressed the rule of 'kinds' but we don't know for sure how or when or where. We can only say that we relied and trusted in other people in a way that only You deserve.

Therefore Father, I repent of giving anyone in authority the kind of trust I should give only to You. I repent of relying on others for information and delegating my responsibility to them, deciding it was too hard to be accountable for the stewardship You have entrusted to me. But I can never evade accountability, Lord. Forgive me for the times I've been negligent—and not searched the Scriptures, not inquired of Your Holy Spirit, not sought the confirmation of two or three independent witnesses.

Lord, whatever the appeal in these tests and temptations—whether it's a legitimate hunger or thirst, whether it's a summons into my calling that is diabolically close to Your destiny for me, whether it's ambition or fleshly pity, untimely mercy or out-of-line timing—help my heart to be in tune with Your heart and the heart of Jesus, so that I choose rightly. Whenever I find myself trapped in a double-bind with no way out, please show me a way of escape—and help me see it at just the right time.

In the name of Jesus, Your Holy Son. Amen.

5

The Cornerstone and the Cloud

God's instructions for Sukkot, the Festival of Tabernacles, or Feast of Booths, are repeated through the Torah. A summary appears in the Book of Leviticus:

> *On the fifteenth day of the seventh month the Lord's Festival of Tabernacles begins, and it lasts for seven days. The first day is a sacred assembly; do no regular work. For seven days present food offerings to the Lord, and on the eighth day hold a sacred assembly.*
>
> Leviticus 23:34–36 NIV

A significant aspect of the holiday is added in Deuteronomy—the command to rejoice at this time:

> *Celebrate the Festival of Tabernacles for seven days after you have gathered the produce of your threshing floor and your winepress. Be joyful at your festival—you, your sons and daughters, your male and female servants, and the Levites, the foreigners, the fatherless and the widows.*
>
> Deuteronomy 16:13–14 NIV

But the close detail is spelled out in Numbers:

> *On the fifteenth day of the seventh month, hold a sacred assembly and do no regular work. Celebrate a festival to the Lord for seven days. Present as an aroma pleasing to the Lord a food offering consisting of a burnt offering of **thirteen** young bulls, two rams and fourteen male lambs a year old, all without defect. With each of the thirteen bulls offer a grain offering of three-tenths of an ephah of the finest flour mixed with oil; with each of the two rams, two-tenths; and with each of the fourteen lambs, one-tenth. Include one male goat as a sin offering, in addition to the regular burnt offering with its grain offering and drink offering.*
>
> *On the second day offer **twelve** young bulls...*
>
> *On the third day offer **eleven** bulls...*
>
> *On the fourth day offer **ten** bulls...*
>
> *On the fifth day offer **nine** bulls...*
>
> *On the sixth day offer **eight** bulls...*
>
> *On the seventh day offer **seven** bulls...*
>
> *On the eighth day hold a closing special assembly and do no regular work. Present as an aroma pleasing to the Lord a food offering consisting of a burnt offering of **one** bull, one ram and seven male lambs a year old, all without defect. With*

the bull, the ram and the lambs, offer their grain offerings and drink offerings according to the number specified.

Numbers 29:12–37 NIV

Basically the offerings are exactly the same for each day, except for the number of bulls. On the seven days of the feast proper, that count of bulls totals 70. Because of the long-standing tradition that the world was divided into 70 nations, that aspect of the Feast is now seen as Israel's sin offering on behalf of the Gentiles.

For their closest neighbours during much of their history—the Canaanites—this time of year was the new wine festival. The Jews, however, established a tradition of water libation. During the Joyous Water-Drawing Ceremony a priest went with a golden pitcher to the Pool of Siloam, filled it and took it through the Water Gate into the Temple where it was poured over the altar with wine from a bowl. This ritual was accompanied by joyful shouts and blasts on the shofar.[38]

Water and wine. Remind you of anything? It should be no surprise that Jesus' first miracle—where water from a pitcher was drawn out as wine—occurred during the Canaanite festival of new wine and the Jewish feast of Sukkot. Wine symbolised joy, celebration, festivity, community and the blessings of God.[39] The wedding feast at Cana embodied all these elements.

The following year, when Sukkot came around again, Jesus was in Jerusalem. On the last and greatest day of the Feast, He stood up and cried out:

> *If anyone thirsts, let him come to Me and drink. The one believing in Me, as the Scripture has said: 'Out of his belly will flow rivers of living water.' Now He said this concerning the Spirit, whom those having believed in Him were about to receive; for the Spirit was not yet given, because Jesus was not yet glorified.*
>
> John 7:37–39 BLB

On this final day, the 'Hoshana Raba', *Great Salvation*, Jesus proclaimed Himself as the Living Water, indicating the Joyous Water-Drawing Ceremony symbolised the Holy Spirit.

Many recent translations substitute another word or phrase for 'belly': *heart, innermost being, deep within, side*. The original Greek actually is *belly*. Our gut brain (yes, we do indeed have a brain there!) is where traumatic memory is stored. Jesus, in talking about a thirst for salvation, is linking it to faith in Himself as the Living Water, the gift of the Holy Spirit and living water that flows from those healed of trauma through that gift.

Trauma and abuse are inextricably linked.

During a third Sukkot, Jesus was at Mount Hermon. Water libation is linked to that locality. In the Book of Jubilees, another text highly regarded during Jesus' lifetime, the time period in which the angelic incursion occurred is mentioned. The usual translation is: 'in the days of Jared.' This is usually understood as meaning the angels descended to Mount Hermon during the time when Jared, the father of Enoch and the great-great-great-grandson of Adam, was alive. However Jared, whose name aptly means *descent*, lived 962 years. This hardly narrows the time parameters.

Derek Gilbert, drawing on the work of archaeologist Charles Clermont-Ganneau, points out that a likely more accurate translation of these words in Jubilees may be that the angels descended 'in the days of the *yarid* [jared]'. Instead of Jared being a person, it is a water-drawing and pouring ceremony. This rite, hydrophory, was practised throughout the ancient world, and 'consisted chiefly in drawing water, which was borne in procession and thrown into a sacred tank.'[40] Sounds seriously like a variation on that Joyous Water-Drawing Ceremony, right? I'd be very deeply concerned about the practice, except for the fact Jesus used it to point to Himself as the Living Water.

Belial and his celestial allies were apparently able to *yarid* to earth through some sort of portal-opening ceremony involving a drink offering to angels. The stone bowl carved into the summit of Mount Hermon may have served as a sacred cup on 'the threshing floor of El'. I believe Gilbert's analysis is right and 'the yarid' was a water libation. I conclude this for no other reason than that Jesus linked Himself with water-drawing *twice* during Sukkot.

However there's one important aspect of this festival that has a bearing on the Transfiguration. And it's the reason God told the people to build booths in the first place.

> *You are to dwell in booths for seven days. All the native-born of Israel must dwell in booths, so that your descendants may know that I made the Israelites dwell in booths when I brought them out of the land of Egypt. I am the Lord your God.*
>
> Leviticus 23:42–43 BSB

Read it again, bearing in mind that a booth—or tabernacle or shelter—is a temporary hut partially shaded by leafy branches. Now ask yourself: when was this supposed to have occurred? During the wilderness years? *Really?* Exactly when did the Lord compel the Israelites to give up their tents?

There's no evidence it ever happened. However—to this day—observant Jews have faithfully followed the command to build a flimsy wooden structure with a partially covered top and to live in it for seven days. Thus they celebrate Sukkot, the time of joy and rest.

Jeremy Chance Springfield points out the solution to this enigma is found in the root meaning of 'sukkah', *partial shade*.[41] I believe that *thin covering* is probably slightly better nuancing. A cloud qualifies as *partial shade* or *thin covering*. So does a leafy bower.

Thus when God said, *'I made the Israelites dwell in booths,'* He was essentially saying, 'They tabernacled with Me under My Cloud.' This was the Cloud of God's glory that guarded and guided the people throughout their wanderings.

Notice how Simon Peter, completely befuddled by the appearance of Moses and Elijah on Mount Hermon, nevertheless has enough sense of propriety about the timing to suggest building tabernacles. And as he does, a bright Cloud overshadows them all and a Voice speaks from the Cloud, saying:

> *This is My Son, whom I love; with Him I am well pleased. Listen to Him!*
>
> Matthew 17:5 NIV

This Cloud comes to the protection of all those on the mountaintop, shielding them from the malice of the war council taking place there. However, I also think there was a certain level of protection in the sheer ineptness of the disciples. The principalities must have been falling over themselves with riotous laughter at Jesus arriving with Peter, James and John in tow. 'You're back? And this is the *best* You've got? These wonder-boys are Your chosen deputies?'

If only they could have seen a few short weeks into the future, they might have been less scornful. They might have reconsidered undermining a time of rapturous joy with their sardonic mockery.

Laughter is associated with thresholds from the time that God announced to Abraham, during a threshold covenant, that he'd have a son named Isaac, *he laughs.*

It's a recurrent theme in Scripture that laughter, either in rejoicing or in mockery, occurs on thresholds. In some mysterious way, laughter is connected to this covering cloud of glory.

The modern rabbinic word for *third heaven* is actually related to the name Isaac. That might seem extremely odd, until we realise that Isaac does not only mean *he laughs* but is a pun on *lintel* or *overhang*. A lintel is that part of a doorway above our heads—one of the places painted with blood at the Passover. A lintel is also, in a sense, a thin overhead covering.

A sukkah, a booth, too is built to have a thin overhead covering. A cloud likewise is a thin overhead covering. And because the cloud in the wilderness years was God's presence of glory, that's what the Feast of Sukkot was about—and also, of course, honour, since glory and honour are entwined in Hebrew thinking—as well as protection.

God's tabernacle is about spreading a table in the presence of your enemies and saying, 'Don't worry about it! Rejoice! Be at rest. I've got you covered. All is well.'

Belial so deeply wants to fake this thin covering, to counterfeit it so you'll be exposed rather than shielded, to substitute his blanket that's not only thin, but far too thin, and that is, in addition, impregnated with poison and virulent disease. The spirit of abuse wants to ensure the Chief Cornerstone and the Cloud of Glory are never genuinely activated in your life. He wants you to keep your own irreparably cracked cornerstone and your pathetically self-patched covering so you can never have safe refuge from him or his *shedim*.

The Cornerstone is designed to be the *covering* beneath you—that's what the Hebrew means—and the Cloud is the covering above you.[42] Both coverings are about covenant and about atonement. The first relates to threshold covenant and the second to name covenant. If you have both these protective elements, as well as the Armour of God around you, the Fruit of the Spirit within you and the Holy Spirit as your paraclete beside you, you can rest and rejoice—just as God commands you to do. You have entered His rest.

Things go wrong because we rely on our own protective measures. Amongst the most famous words of Jesus regarding faith are:

> *If you have faith as small as a mustard seed, you can say to this mountain, 'Move from here to there,' and it will move. Nothing will be impossible for you.*
>
> Matthew 17:20 NIV

The mountain He was talking about was actually Mount Hermon, because this statement occurred right after His return from the top. And really, He wasn't—and isn't—talking about a mustard seed's worth of faith flinging the mountain itself to one side or even into the sea. He was talking about what the mountain represents. It symbolises every principality and power along with every demonic agenda. That's what we can move by faith. By tabernacling within the Cloud and having it as our guard and guide.

Now one of the most significant aspects of God's announcement from the Cloud of Glory is that His words are those of a midwife.[43] This might be surprising but it shouldn't be. After all, this is the mountain, where the Watchers took oaths to mate with suitable women—their agenda being to wreck God's redemptive plan by interfering with the genetics of the human race. This involved the conception and birth of children.

The plan for redemption has to include an overturning of that spiritual payload involving what it means to be counted amongst the 'children of God'. Jesus totally reversed this history of the mountain. Just as a woman conceives through a fertilised egg, which is then implanted in her womb and is nurtured through pregnancy to a birth nine months later, so through the actions of Jesus we find a parallel for the church.

'On this rock, I will build My church,' He said. On this cornerstone, in fact. This was the moment of conception, there in the shadow of Mount Hermon at Caesarea Philippi. Words of identity were fertilised by words of faith. But unless a fertilised egg is implanted within six to eight days, it will naturally abort. It was on Hermon's summit six days later that the church was implanted

through the midwifery of God's words—and it was around eight and a half months later that the church was born at Pentecost.

Once we realise this timing then we are able to look back and see that the Watchers knew enough about God's plan for redemption to try to pre-empt the overshadowing work of the Holy Spirit. As Mary conceived Jesus, the fully-human fully-divine Son of God, so the daughters of mankind conceived human-divine hybrids through union with the 'bene ha-Elohim', traditionally interpreted as *sons of God*.

Through covenantal oneness with Jesus we not only become children of God, but we're called to replace the governmental rule of the seventy principalities. It's no coincidence that, not long after descending the mountain and collecting His disciples, Jesus organised a mission for them. He paired them up and then sent seventy of them out on a ministry journey through Samaria and Galilee. And just so those seventy principalities back on the mountain got the message loud and clear He sent the seventy disciples not to the big towns but to the *small villages*—'kephir' in Hebrew—a word that also means *young lions*. As it happened, Young Lions was a title for those seventy angel-princes on Mount Hermon.

Is it any wonder that during this time Jesus saw the satan fall like lightning from heaven? I don't doubt it was to check out how it was possible for divine light to be spreading so fast through a land that had been spiritually dark for centuries. Jesus couldn't possibly be doing it—as a human, He couldn't be in all those places at once.

The principalities might have laughed at those three seeming dunderheads Jesus took with Him to the mountaintop but, within days, they were healing the sick and casting out demons wherever they went. They had become a massive, unstoppable threat.

I used to think the Transfiguration was *just* Jesus pointing out He really was God! Now let me assure you there is even more going on during that event than I've mentioned so far. Much much more.

But my point is to show the importance of the right covering—both Cornerstone and Cloud. Jesus gives us a blueprint for how to counteract the spirit of abuse during the three times He celebrated Sukkot during His ministry.

One of the purposes of abuse—from the point of view of the spirit behind it—is to change DNA. This is not just to befoul God's creation, it's also to create 'fit extensions'— just as was case back in the day when the Watchers saw that the daughters of Adam were 'fair'.

Since the advent of research into epigenetics, we know that trauma can result in changes to DNA—a kind of superstructure can impose itself on genes that lasts for three or four generations. I have to suspect that this is the physical mechanism by which the spirit of abuse seeks to create fit extensions for itself and its progeny, who are now demons.

It's normally trauma through which demons opportunistically gain a foothold of access into people's lives. But they don't want just a toehold, they want a stronghold. Through mind control, through a siege on those portions of our souls holding a line of resistance, Belial wants to make us a fit receptacle for possession—a temporary tabernacle for one or more of the wandering spirits who are his demonic offspring. He needs a booth to park them in while he diligently works at discovering how God made that resurrection thing to fly—so he can bring his sons back. Belial knows it can be done—Yahweh, after all, brought His Son back.

In the meantime, it's always, always, always about the counterfeit. There is no originality, no creative spark from the enemies of God; they continually copy His plans and His purposes, pre-empting Him with timing, trying to create scenarios where His word cannot be fulfilled. Because if they could do that, then it would be possible to depose Him. If God ever breaks any of His promises, it would be possible for His opponents to challenge His rule and take His throne from Him.[44] He would then have to do their bidding.

These are the high stakes involved.

It might seem like it's all too hard for us to be overcomers. It seems Belial has got it all covered. But I think there's another reason why Jesus took three particularly dull-minded disciples to the war council of the spirit abusers who control the government of nations. It encourages us to realise we don't have to know what we're doing. It helps… but the main thing is just to be with Him.

God has given us incredibly simple tools to dismantle those 'fit extensions' that trauma builds as a scaffold on our DNA: forgiveness, repentance, renunciation.

But all too often we decide to rely on a declaration using our delegated authority—forgetting such decrees are completely undermined by lack of forgiveness or repentance, failure to honour, fortification of our false refuges or complicity with the enemy through vows, covenants and internal belief systems.

We have to govern ourselves before we are ready to be given authority over others. A major motif of Sukkot, hidden below the obvious themes of joy, laughter, rest, tabernacles and clouds is reconciliation with the nations.

Those seventy bulls sacrificed during Sukkot are seen as applying, not to Israel, but on behalf of the nations. That hydrophory, that water-drawing ceremony, that libation mirroring and inverting 'the yarid' that called down the Watchers, may be symbolically connected to dominion of the earth. Chaim Bentorah points out that Christian scholars teach that the Hebrew word, 'yiredu', for *dominion* comes from the root 'radah' which means *to exert control over* or *overpower*. However rabbinic teachers suggest it comes from 'yarad', *to descend, to lower oneself and show respect.* Scripture teaches respect for creation, Bentorah points out, not control of it.[45]

The 'jared' and 'yarad' are identical words. And if *dominion* really means *showing respect for*, then it may well be the case that whoever performed the yarid water libation and called the Watchers down may simply have made a tragic mistake.[46] A misguided act of honour opened a gateway for an angelic beachhead. Now, this may be a misinterpretation of the situation—there may have been intentional worship of angels along with an invitation for them to intervene on earth. But my point is that this doesn't need to be the case. Humanity has a habit of charging ahead, blissfully ignorant of any long-term dangers and dismissing all but immediate potential hazards. So, with regard to the yarid, I think we can safely assess it as negligence—yes, definitely. Malice—probably unlikely.

Yet the abuse of children has gone on since that time. The Watchers descended to Mount Hermon to create children. Jesus ascended to Mount Hermon to create a child—His church—born through the Holy Spirit in the following year fifty days after Passover. The Watchers wanted children who could not be redeemed under the promises made by God to Adam and Eve. Jesus was the fulfilment of the promise of God for a redeemer for mankind. The Watchers wanted their descendants to have complete dominion over both the earth and the human genome: so that no 'pure humans' would exist any longer. Jesus wanted His church to be a governing body with dominion of the world—respect for it—

through preaching the gospel, overturning unjust social and political structures, casting out demons and healing those who are sick, abused, bound or traumatised.

It's always about the children when Belial is part of the picture. The very first thing that happens when Jesus comes down the mountain after the Transfiguration is that He heals a child, suffering from epilepsy—but also, incidentally, from spiritual abuse.

In the ancient world, epilepsy was known as *panolepsy* and was considered as possession by the goat-god called Pan by the Greeks and Azazel by the Jews. Each year, on Yom Kippur, a goat was chosen by lot to send to Azazel, the scapegoat.

Now the father who met Jesus at Caesarea Philippi might have had all the best intentions in the world—but he was about to compound the boy's problems, not relieve them. His inadvertent spiritual abuse would have opened the door to Azazel's close ally, Belial.

> *A man came up to Jesus and knelt before Him. 'Lord, have mercy on my son,' he said. 'He has seizures and is suffering terribly. He often falls into the fire or into the water. I brought him to Your disciples, but they could not heal him.'*
>
> *'O unbelieving and perverse generation!' Jesus replied. 'How long must I remain with you? How*

long must I put up with you? Bring the boy here to Me.' Then Jesus rebuked the demon, and it came out of the boy, and he was healed from that moment.

Afterward the disciples came to Jesus privately and asked, 'Why couldn't we drive it out?'

'Because you have so little faith,' He answered. 'For truly I tell you, if you have faith the size of a mustard seed, you can say to this mountain, "Move from here to there," and it will move. Nothing will be impossible for you.'

Matthew 17:14–20 BSB

Many people think that the words, *'O unbelieving and perverse generation!',* are directed to the disciples. They are clearly directed at the father. Remember that Jesus has just come down the mountain after the Transfiguration. He has rejoined His disciples and therefore, although the location is not mentioned, it is evident He has returned to Caesarea Philippi. He is back in the vicinity of the temple precinct near the shrine of Pan and the Gates of Hell. And there can be only one reason a father with a son troubled by epilepsy would be at that particular locale: he would be there to make a sacrifice to Pan for the release of his son.

Jesus was rightly angry—but we can feel for the desperate father. He'd obviously suffered a catastrophic loss of faith. But that doesn't make his action any less perverse—and that's the point of Jesus' words. You can't have compassion on perversity. If you do, you become complicit with it. The father was willing to make a sacrifice—to covenant with Pan. That would not have released his son. It would have bound uncounted generations from that point on to a goat-god specialising in panic, rejection and lust. Just the sort of gifts you want your son and his sons and their sons to carry with them throughout their lives! And this abuse would then have opened the way for a secondary infestation by Belial.

This is the context in which Jesus tells His disciples that only a mustard-seed of faith is needed to not only move the mountain claimed by Belial *'from here to there'* but all his cronies and supporters as well. And this shows us that the opposition of Jesus towards Belial was relentless.

Timing is both critical—and unimportant. That's the paradox of what He showed us.

During the Sukkot when the wedding feast at Cana was celebrated, the wine ran out. When Mary told Jesus, His response was: *'My hour has not yet come.'* (John 2:4 BSB)

The time was not right.

Nonetheless, He directed the servants to pour water and draw it and, in a miracle, in a supernatural Joyous Water-Drawing Ceremony, water did more than mix with wine—it *became* wine.

Six days prior to the wedding, it had been Yom Kippur and Jesus had been out in the wilderness, facing the temptations of the satan. He'd refused to change stone into bread, to perform an act of magic and change 'kinds'. But isn't changing water into wine a changing of 'kinds'? Not at all. Jesus later said:

'I do nothing of Myself; but as My Father taught Me.'
John 8:28 NKJV

The point is that changing water into wine is exactly what God does every day along grape vines. Water and trace minerals, along with sunlight to ignite the fuse of photosynthesis, combine to make a grape, the source of wine. Yet instead of taking months for the grape clusters to grow and years for the wine to mature, the miracle of Jesus changed both time and timing. He was not just showing Himself to us as the 'True Vine' in this instance, thereby slamming the claims of Dionysius-Zagreus to that title,[47] He was showing Himself as the true Lord of Time.

The prophet Daniel spoke of a king who would oppose the Ancient of Days, and

speak against the Most High and oppress His holy people and try to change the set times.
Daniel 7:25 NIV

The spirit of abuse who has another face as the spirit of time continually seeks to counterfeit the work of the Lord of Time and Eternity, Jesus of Nazareth.[48]

During the Sukkot when Jesus was in Jerusalem and got up on the last and greatest day of the feast to proclaim Himself as the Living Water, the displaced time elements are very subtle. This was the day of 'Hoshana Raba', *the Great Salvation*, and to actually recognise Jesus' claim as the Living Water, it would have been appropriate at this time to start waving fronds cut from palm trees while shouting 'Hosanna!'

This did finally happen, of course, but it was in the week before Passover in the *following*[49] year—some eighteen or nineteen months, at least, in the future. Once again, timing is a subtle background feature of what Jesus was doing.

However, from a practical point of view, the most important action of Jesus is His quote from Scripture:

> *'Out of his belly will flow rivers of living water.'*
> John 7:38 BLB

Where does this verse come from? It doesn't appear anywhere in our present canon. Perhaps it's not a quote at all, and the words of Jesus, *'as the Scripture has said,'* actually should be appended to His statement immediately prior to this:

> *'If anyone thirsts, let him come to Me and drink.'*
> John 7:37 ESV

Even that is not an exact quote but is a slightly tinkered version of Isaiah's prophecy:

> *'Come, all you who are thirsty, come to the waters.'*
> Isaiah 55:1 NIV

Jesus, as was His normal practice, showed how prophecy—and also the Torah, teachings and even tradition—pointed to Him. In fact, once we think about it, even the great rebellion of the Watcher angels points to Him in a back-to-front way.

My view is that *'Out of his belly will flow rivers of living water'* is effectively a commentary by Jesus on Isaiah. John then provides us with further commentary to explain it's about the Holy Spirit. The closest thought to these words of Jesus comes from Proverbs:

> *Keep your heart with all diligence, for out of it is the wellspring of life.*
>
> Proverbs 4:23 WEB

Here *wellspring* has the sense of a *boundary*—the very thing that is constantly violated by those designated as 'sons of Belial'. There is a reference to a 'daughter of Belial', so women should not feel either left out, or safe, for that matter. No other threshold spirit is mentioned in Scripture as having sons—well, Leviathan is, but it's unclear whether the 'sons of pride' are human or angelic, and personally I think the unusual word for *pride* is a reference to the *young lions* of Mount Hermon, which are not Belial's Watchers but principalities. Belial appears to be alone in acquiring a family of human sons and daughters.

God gives us boundaries, asks us to put them in place and then guard them. The Hebrew word behind Sukkot, 'sukkah', *small temporary tabernacle* or *booth*, not only has a sense of a *thin covering* but also has the sense of a *thicket* or *fence, a protective boundary*. It is similar to *wellspring* in meaning. Thus it makes perfect sense for Jesus to refer to wellsprings of Living Water on Sukkot—there's a natural alignment of thought even though the words are different. What He's really talking about is proper restoration of boundaries.

But sometimes, when we've been influenced by Belial to invert truth, we put boundaries in place to keep hurt in and healing out.

This is where the precise words of Jesus, *'Out of his belly will flow rivers of living water,'* become so significant. There's no question He used the word *belly*, not *heart.* This means that, if He was referring to Proverbs 4:23, He clarified the wording. And this is important because the memory of trauma is stored in the gut brain, not in the head brain or the heart brain. Until recently, the prevailing scientific understanding was that the gut was simply part of the digestive system. We were not aware there is a brain actually residing in the gut, even though people spoke of 'being gutted' and 'gut instinct' and 'gut-wrenching'. Ordinary everyday experience was ignored in favour of 'settled' science. The brain in the gut is in charge of emotions. The brain in our head is our cognitive centre while our gut brain is the emotional centre.

Ultimately, when it comes to trauma, the gut holds the key to release. The brain in the belly is stuck in the past, causing abused people to always talk in past tense, not in present tense. The emotional brain is unable to move on, because *now* is, to it, the past.

Jesus didn't just talk about 'living water' at Sukkot. The first time He did so was when He encountered a woman at a well in Samaria—a woman who was five times married, belonged to a despised ethnic group and seemed to be marginalised within her own town. It doesn't take any imagination to realise she would have been seriously traumatised emotionally and spiritually, if not in other ways as well. The 'living water' Jesus promised her included, among other things, emotional and spiritual healing.

Thus the gift of living water from the belly of Jesus is the gift of healing to our bellies—to the gut brain with its reservoir of emotional and spiritual trauma.

It doesn't matter how desperately the mind says, 'I want healing,' if the heart and belly present a solid united front to keep up that wellspring with its reversed boundary, it's not going to happen. The borders of our lives might look like a rickety tumbledown fence from the point of view of abusers who trample on it, but from anyone else's perspective—and that includes the self—they are shieldwalls topped with jagged glass and electric wire. No one gets permission to pass. No one. The only reason abusers so frequently cross the line is because they never ask for permission.

The mind can therefore seek healing for decades but traumatic memory is not stored there. It may not even be stored in the belly—but the gut brain has a library file that knows where in the body the memory has been placed. It's necessary to command the gut to allow Jesus to pour living water from His belly—the seat of divine emotional memory—to heal our own emotional memory.

The mind therefore has to take authority and, using the will, speak to the heart and the gut to tell them to open a gate or door in that boundary. Allow the Living Water of Jesus and the Holy Spirit to flow into both the memory of the trauma and the physical, emotional and spiritual effects of the trauma. This does not require a reliving of the trauma or even bringing up the memory of the trauma—just permission to access the library file so that Jesus and the Holy Spirit can wash it clean with Living Water and restore the boundaries so that they begin to keep healing in and hurt out.

If it all sounds too wacky—perhaps because you've never heard of the gut brain or heart brain before—simply ask Jesus of Nazareth this question: Is this what I need to do for healing? Is this what You want for me?

Preparation

Hold one of your hands on your head. Place the other hand on your belly. This is to let your body know that, while your mind is going to be directing your heart and your belly, nevertheless this is intended to be a unified, cooperative action. Your cognitive centre is requesting the emotional brain in the gut to put aside fear and to be involved in healing along with every part of the self—encompassing heart, soul, mind and body.

Choose a traumatic incident. Allow your mind to pick out of its memory banks an incident from the past. It doesn't necessarily have to involve abuse. You do not have to recall any of the details of the event, just provide a suitable label for it—for example, *'The Night of the Accident.'*

Now from the mind to the belly and the heart, make this request:

'Belly, you are the seat of my emotional brain. Heart, you hold the keys of grief. Together, you have a filing system that records where in my body the memory of *The Night of the Accident* is stored. I come with Jesus. I do not require you to remember. But I ask you to give Jesus access to the memory's place of storage. I ask you to lower the boundary that keeps hurt in and healing out. I ask you to unlock the gate to allow Jesus in. I want your cooperation. Choose healing with me now, right now, and allow Him in as the Living Water and allow the Holy Spirit to flow through the file and into the muscle or organ where the pain is stored. Together with me, choose a washing and cleansing of the memory so it is no longer a harm to us all, but becomes a source of healing for others.'

Prayer

Heavenly Father, You have heard me choose Jesus as the Living Water. Help my belly to open the gate to healing. My head and my heart want it, but my belly is so used to keeping me safe by locking the pain away that it needs help to choose life and to agree to allowing the memories stored in my muscles and organs to receive the Water of the Wellspring of Life. Lord, please line up my belly with the belly of Jesus so that His Living Water can flow full and free into that file I have labelled and selected. Please restore me—every part of me—to the design You have always wanted for me.

Where trauma from past generations has affected my DNA and erected an epigenetic scaffold on it, please remove any access points or extensions that would allow demonic attachment. If there is demonic attachment already in place, show me what I need to do, if anything, to remove it. If there is nothing I need to do other than ask You to detach it, then I'm asking right now, this very moment.

I forgive those who have ignored my boundaries and poisoned my wellsprings, yet I also repent of developing the expectation that people would not accept my right to say 'no'. I repent therefore of remaining silent when I could have spoken up, and thus of allowing people to trample on my boundaries and defile my wellsprings. I ask You to provide me with the wisdom and understanding to guard my heart, as well as mind and belly, rightly and effectively from this point on. Help me too to become a reservoir of the Living Water of Jesus Christ so that I can pass on the blessings of His healing to others.

In His Name. Amen.

6

We Have Met the Enemy...

BEFORE EVER I HAD A NAME for the spirit of abuse, I could nevertheless see its hoofprint in Scripture quite clearly. The story that first screamed to me that this spirit was in some way connected with thresholds was that mysterious episode at the beginning of the second book of Samuel. Saul has just died in battle—but who was going to inherit the throne was unclear. The people of Judah were following the giant-killing hero from their own tribe, David, while the rest of the Israelites were loyal to Ish-bosheth, the forty-year old surviving son of Saul of the tribe of Benjamin.

David had his capital at Hebron, and Ish-bosheth had moved to the far side of the Jordan, to Mahanaim, near the place where Jacob had wrestled with the angel. Now both kings had their warbands. David's armies were led by his volatile nephew Joab. Ish-bosheth's were under the command of his cousin Abner. Clearly the business of leading a king's army was a family affair. Rather surprisingly, despite supporting different candidates for the kingship and effectively being on opposite sides of the political fence, Joab and Abner seem to have been friends—at least up until the time of a very peculiar incident that occurred near the Pool of Gibeon.

What happened was this: Joab with a battalion from Judah in tow had ranged into the territory of Benjamin and headed for Gibeon, previously a Philistine garrison town.[50] They reached it just as Abner came marching up with his own troop of men. The armies proceeded to take up positions on either side of the Pool of Gibeon. Abner then suggested they have a game. A *laugh*. That's his exact word in Hebrew. I doubt I would have considered it significant, even after I noticed the utter strangeness of this episode, except for the fact that I was beginning to see a pattern involving *laughter at thresholds*. Sometimes it was happy laughter, but often it was contempt and mockery. It was difficult to understand why joy on the one hand and derision on the other should be associated with thresholds, but the examples of both kept multiplying.

Anyway, Abner's idea of a laugh on this particular occasion was to have twelve young men from each of the different armies line up in pairs, grab each other by the hair and shove a sword into their opponent's side. Joab, unbelievably, agrees to this bizarre sporting contest. Not unnaturally, it didn't end well.

And suddenly, it's as if both sides wake up from a collective trance and realise their friends have just been sacrificed for a laugh. Yes, here laid out in Scripture, there's an incredible example of group mind control.

What on earth was lurking at the Pool of Gibeon? What could induce this sort of fatal misjudgment and amnesia on the part of two army commanders about the consequences of playing with sharp, pointy objects?

Now we don't find out about Gibeon's backstory or how its landscape came to be defiled for another nineteen chapters. But we do find out that, having awoken with shock from their stupor and taken stock of the death of the comrades, the armies of David and Ish-bosheth didn't find the laugh particularly amusing. They immediately started to attack each other. Abner, quite wisely in my view, made a run for it. However he was spotted and followed by Joab's fleet-footed brother, Asahel.

Abner called out repeatedly, trying to dissuade Asahel from the pursuit but his warnings were ignored. Abner then turned and put a spear through Asahel, killing him and setting in motion yet another round of tit-for-tat vengeance in the centuries-old feud between the people of Bethlehem and the people of Gibeah. Although Abner got away and later defected to David's side, thereby handing the kingship of all the tribes into David's hands, Joab nursed a grudge over his brother's death. He conspired to lure Abner out from sanctuary in one of the cities of refuge and he murdered him in retaliation. David's response on hearing the news was quite odd: he not only wept, but made a song of lament for Abner. Probably this was not the wisest political move since it insulted and demeaned Joab as the avenger of blood.

Now both Abner and Joab, the principal players throughout this strange episode with all its subtle overtones of ritual sacrifice, both have 'ab', *father*, in their name. Those twelve pairs of young men seemed to be killing each other as stand-ins and representatives of the 'father'. Before I had the name 'Belial' to attach to the spirit of abuse—hidden as it was beneath a translation of *scoundrels* or *worthless fellows*—I could nevertheless see in this episode that it was associated with armies and a desire to kill the father. So as I went looking for a word that fitted this idea, I came across the notion of the Janissary. And so 'Janissary spirit' became my working handle while I continued my search for the Scriptural name of this spirit.

'Janissary' aptly denoted an army spirit with a hatred of the father and of fatherhood. The meaning, *new troops,* and the job description, 'guardians of the Sublime Porte', fitted a threshold spirit that has turned against all our divine Father stands for and is intent on turning the hearts of the children towards killing their parents and destroying all they've worked towards. It's a spirit that tempts us to hate all fathers and authority figures, and to fracture our society. Its pervasive influence is accelerating through our culture. When Belial gets into a church environment, it not only tempts some people to commit abuse, it tempts others to defend the abusers and reject the victims.

In the story of Joab and Abner, its ally is Lilith, the vampire spirit—the one who stakes, spears or stabs. We see this with the young men sacrificed, as well as with

Asahel, whose name means *God has made*. Behind it all is an attack on God's creation.

Another strong ally of Belial is the spirit of rejection and panic, Azazel. Rejection and abuse simply work well together. So does Leviathan, the spirit of retaliation, and Ziz, the spirit of forgetting and truth-tearing.

Now nineteen chapters later in the second book of Samuel, we are finally handed the clues as to why something dark and malevolent was lurking in the vicinity of the Pool of Gibeon. During David's reign there had been a drought for three years and famine was ravaging the land. Inquiring of the Lord, he discovered that it was because Saul had massacred almost all of the Gibeonites—who, although they were Canaanites, were to have been protected under the covenant they'd made with Joshua and the people of Israel centuries previously. Saul, no doubt, was in a very difficult situation—Gibeon was a Philistine outpost. So the Gibeonites were playing fast and loose with the covenant themselves. Nonetheless, clearly this did not excuse Saul's actions.

His own hometown of Gibeah had been the site of a genocide a generation or two previously. According to the law,[51] after its destruction, it should never have been rebuilt. It appears, however, that Saul decided the way around this was simply to rename it—from Gibeah of Benjamin to Gibeah of Saul—after himself naturally—and this would circumvent the problem of God's law prohibiting any rebuilding and reoccupation.[52]

Now remember Gibeah had been the place where the concubine had died as a result of abuse by the 'sons of Belial'. That spirit was so firmly entrenched in the landscape that Saul, through his re-establishment of the city, brought defilement on himself. He was therefore tempted to re-create the very same sort of genocide that had so traumatised the people of Benjamin for generations—Belial, after all, wants the abuse to go on.

Saul fell for the temptation. The parallels between the two genocides are so strong that even the names, Gibeah and Gibeon, have the same meaning. While most English translations render them simply as *rocky hill*, I believe this should be nuanced as *rocky hill shaped like an upturned bowl or cup*.[53] Without the slightest research support, just a nagging intuition that refuses to be dismissed, I believe these particular hills were often designated as locations for ritual activity and were associated with a cup of blessing or a cup of suffering.

David, on being tested in turn when the Gibeonites ask for revenge against the House of Saul, added to the trauma in the land. Yet ever so appropriately, given the events that allowed Belial to set all this feuding and abuse in train for generations and centuries, it was a concubine's actions that brought a measure of healing to the land. Rizpah, Saul's concubine, awakened David's conscience to the dishonour and suffering he was continuing to inflict on the land. He wasn't solving the crisis of the drought, he was actually making it worse.

Most English Bibles make it difficult to find the incidents involving Belial. Having decided that 'Belial' doesn't have any supernatural overtones but means *worthless* or *without profit*, translators usually render the phrase for followers of this spirit as *worthless fellows*. Instead of 'sons of Belial' or 'daughters of Belial', we read *troublemakers* or *scoundrels*. This completely obscures their allegiance to a specific unholy godling and generally trivialises the perverse overtones of the situation where the phrase is used. However, by looking at the patterns of usage, we can see Belial is associated not only with abuse but with perversity, depravity, violence, false accusation and with wild chaotic armies. We can also uncover its allies and come to acknowledge our own complicity.

The first time Belial is mentioned in relation to abuse is in the opening chapters of the book of 1 Samuel. Hannah had gone with her husband to Shiloh where Eli and his sons were ministering before the Ark of the Covenant. It transpires that Eli's sons were scoundrels. In the original Hebrew, as I hope you suspect, that's 'sons of Belial'.

> *They had no regard for the Lord. Now it was the practice of the priests that, whenever any of the people offered a sacrifice, the priest's servant would come with a three-pronged fork in his*

hand while the meat was being boiled and would plunge the fork into the... pot. Whatever the fork brought up the priest would take for himself... Even before the fat was burned, the priest's servant would come and say to the person who was sacrificing, 'Give the priest some meat to roast; he won't accept boiled meat from you, but only raw.'

If the person said... 'Let the fat be burned first, and then take whatever you want,' the servant would answer, 'No, hand it over now; if you don't, I'll take it by force.'

This sin of the young men was very great in the Lord's sight, for they were treating the Lord's offering with contempt.

1 Samuel 2:12-17 NIV

The passage then goes on to detail sexual abuse and, of course, spiritual abuse:

Eli, who was very old, heard about everything his sons were doing to all Israel and how they slept with the women who served at the entrance to the tent of meeting. So he said to them, 'Why do you do such things? I hear from all the people about these wicked deeds of yours.'

1 Samuel 2:22-23 NIV

God eventually accused Eli of honouring his sons more than he honoured Yahweh Himself. And He pronounced a curse on the entire bloodline. Destruction followed

Eli's descendants for generations and, ironically, worthless scoundrels destroyed even the righteous and innocent among them.

This is yet another tactic of the spirit of abuse: it wants us to **honour men more than we honour God**. It wants us to set up the conditions for our own destruction by supplanting God and elevating human beings to platforms where their revelation is supreme. And once such leaders assume the throne we give them, we have created the perfect conditions for abuse to flourish.

Scripture tells us to honour everyone[54] but some people today interpret a 'culture of honour' to mean that anyone above us in a hierarchy should never be rebuked. Instead they should receive unqualified respect. However, honour sometimes involves a rebuke. In fact, the Greek word for 'rebuke' means *to render back the honour that is due*.

This is why it's so appropriate to ask the Lord to rebuke Belial or any other threshold spirit. If we receive back in due measure, reaping as we have sown, then for rebuking graciously the worst that can happen is that the Lord will mete back to us the honour we have already exhibited.

It's wise to stick to the guidelines of Scripture. We are told not to bind Leviathan, and I believe that should be the general principle for all threshold guardians. There is no record in Scripture of Jesus binding any demon, though He rebuked plenty and cast them out. In His day, words of binding were associated with occult practices, so we need to use them only at the Lord's direction. If we do not do so, then we may be crossing the line into using the power of the word, a power God infused into declarative speech, against Him. That's magic. It's spell-binding—which is simply using words-of-binding instead of chains—and is what the Watchers taught the women in the days before the flood, according to the Book of Enoch.[55]

Eli went too far with honour by tolerating abuse. Honouring anyone more than we honour God is not just setting ourselves up for destruction but our families too. Society in Eli's time was in serious trouble, on course for a complete wipeout. Just as Belial was foiled in his plan to wreck humanity because of God's intervention through the flood and the rescue of Noah, so again the Lord put into action a plan to save the people crying out to Him.

This time it was a woman who was the agent of grace. Her name was Hannah and, when Eli accused her of being drunk, she was forthright in telling him she was *not* a daughter of Belial. It's clear by her words that she had discerned what spirit was in operation at the sanctuary in Shiloh. And she also knew that Belial is a spirit of armies.

Although it's the father-heart of God that Belial wants to overcome, it's the mother-heart of God that actually overcomes it. As an army spirit, it is a counterfeit of Yahweh Sabaoth, the Lord of Hosts, the God of Angel Armies.

The very first person in Scripture to call the Lord by the name 'Yahweh Sabaoth' was Hannah. And God empowers her against Belial simply by granting her the desire of her heart: motherhood. She becomes the mother of Samuel.

You see, God was in the midst of changing something in Hannah's world and in the society of her time. He was doing the utterly incredible. He was *changing the rules*.

There was an iron-clad rule about who could be the high priest in the Promised Land. No ifs, no buts, no maybes. The person had to be male and had to be a Levite. But that wasn't enough. They also had to be descended from Aaron.

Now God had already changed the rules about the priesthood once before. And this foreshadows what He would do later with Jesus.

Originally every father was a priest in his own household and the firstborn son was the priest for the wider family. But then, as a result of the sin involving the golden calf, when only the Levites rallied to Moses' call to side with God, the Lord said this:

> *'I have taken the Levites in place of all the firstborn sons in Israel.'*
>
> Numbers 8:18 NIV

So the priesthood passed to the Levites—and the high priesthood passed to the sons of Aaron. But that line through Eli had become corrupt. The defilement had infected his bloodline and the nation. So God did something remarkable: He created a situation where a boy would be adopted into Eli's family, into the bloodline of Aaron. But to do that He required Hannah's cooperation.

God never forces us. He asks us.

Otherwise it would be abuse.

God had a long-term plan to get rid of the sons of Eli. They were so corrupt they wielded power over people, even as they were worshipping God. It must have taken decades for God's plans to reach fruition because the problems existed long before Hannah prayed for a son and promised to give him to God to serve in the sanctuary. Then Samuel had to be born, grow up and become old enough to take over the priesthood when all of Eli's family died in a single day.

As I've tried to understand how Belial operates, I've read thousands of articles about the responses of churches to allegations of leaders taking advantage of power. There are many terrible stories out there and no denomination is free from this; no religion either.

Several stories struck me forcibly: one about a woman called to a church where the previous pastor was convicted of sex crimes. She was stunned to find no one ever talked about what had happened. It was so unnatural, she preached a sermon mentioning her own struggles with the wounds of abuse from her childhood. This was a church of just 85 people. In the next week, over two dozen women contacted her about the abuse they had suffered. Some of them were in their eighties and had never spoken about the pain of the secret they'd been keeping almost all their lives.

The second story that struck me forcibly was that of a minister and his wife who protected their son for decades. He had used his position in the church to seduce many vulnerable women during counselling and had also engaged in serious financial impropriety. It reminded me so much of the story of Eli and his sons that I wondered what had happened to this family. Would the curse of the House of Eli, the premature blindness along with innocent lives abruptly cut short, still operate in our own era? The family was sufficiently famous to be able to google them—and truly, the tragedies down the generational line were a genuine echo of the ancient Biblical principle that, if you honour your children more than you honour God, then lives will be cut short.

Now, to be honest, I think for many people there's an even deeper temptation than honouring our children more than we honour God. *Temptation* is probably not the right word. Maybe it's *ordeal*. The choice between honouring our friends and honouring God.

None of us likes to be rejected; none of us likes to lose a friendship, none of us likes to forfeit the acceptance of a colleague. Afraid of rejection, we remain silent when a friend dishonours God. If we've already lost a friend previously because of a rebuke taken poorly, it's not easier to do it a second time, it's much harder. We know the price of honouring God, especially if the friend has a higher status than us in a work or social environment, or the power to cut us off from a wider network of people. Or even cause us to lose our position.

The history of Christianity over the last half century in particular is littered with victims and whistle-blowers who were ignored or who, if they were persistent, had their reputations destroyed through concerted effort. Churches and Christian organisations have a long record of not reporting criminal actions, even when there is a legal requirement to do so. Scripture tells us to submit to the governing authorities but many churches flout the law. Instead they pressure victims to forgive their abusers and to remain in situations where they are in harm's way. If it's a choice between destroying the life of a child and destroying the reputation of a colleague, too many pastoral teams choose the child.

That's not the intention, of course, but it's what repeatedly happens when forgiveness is not accompanied by repentance. And there's a reason why God tells us to separate from those influenced by Belial— as Paul quotes, *'Come out from them and be separate'*[56] —and it's the same reason as the Israelites were to keep away from the destroyed cities where Belial had been worshipped: the opportunity for defilement and corruption simply by being in the vicinity is too great.

Look what happened at the Pool of Gibeon to soldiers just passing through.

This is not to say that Jesus cannot change hearts. However, when repentance only occurs immediately after the abuse is exposed, we should be very, very, very wary. Reserve judgment on whether it's true repentance. It's necessary to remember that abusers are almost always accomplished actors—otherwise they wouldn't get away with what they do for so long.

We have to recognise the enemy as the enemy. We're not fighting against flesh and blood but against the powers of darkness. Yet in this world, we also have to recognise that the complicity of those at the top of our hierarchical structures—however big or small those hierarchies are—is a major enabling factor in reinforcing Belial's stronghold in our midst.

God calls us to deploy goodness, kindness, faithfulness whenever we see the work of Belial around us. Whether it's corruption like that of the sons of Eli, narcissistic self-centredness like foolish Nabal who abused David by accepting his protection but refusing to feed his men, false testimony designed to bring about a person's death like the rogues who accused Naboth of cursing God, God calls us to stand against it.

To defend the defenceless.

Not to defend the indefensible.

So often the perversity of an abusive situation is shown when mercy is offered to the abuser and none to the victim. We are not to turn a blind eye as Eli did; we are not to ignore the cries of the helpless. We are to stand up for what is good, oppose and expose perversity, and keep the law of the land. Forgiveness does not negate justice nor override our responsibility to report crimes.

In this world where children are too soon sexualised, we must carefully weigh their testimonies more than ever. The principle of two or three witnesses should not be overlooked. Though the witnesses don't need to be human, of course. God didn't always use human witnesses, so we can count 'evidence' as witness.

We are to listen. In general, what victims want above all else is to be heard. Heard and heeded. The process of processing is long and arduous. Very few victims want to go to court; they fear to face that trauma; but they want to be heard.

We are to be kind. Abused people need to experience kindness in order to heal. They need to know what blessing looks like.

We are to remember that the ancient law God gave His people said to have nothing to do with the sons of Belial. There's lots of wisdom in that. Until people who are influenced by this spirit are no longer empowered by our unsanctified fleshly mercy, they won't have any incentive to truly repent.

We are to pray without ceasing. We pray to Yahweh Sabaoth, the Lord of Hosts, to keep us undefiled in the midst of a society increasingly influenced by Belial. The song of Hannah to Yahweh Sabaoth is the first prophecy in Scripture to acknowledge that the Lord has a Messiah, an anointed one:

> *'My heart rejoices in the Lord in whom my horn is exalted. My mouth speaks boldly against my enemies, for I rejoice in Your salvation.*
>
> *There is no one holy like the Lord. Indeed, there is no one besides You! And there is no Rock like our God.*
>
> *Do not boast so proudly, or let arrogance come from your mouth, for the Lord is a God who knows*
>
> *...*
>
> *He guards the steps of His faithful ones, but the wicked perish in darkness; for by his own strength shall no man prevail. Those who oppose the Lord will be shattered. He will thunder from heaven against them.*
>
> *The Lord will judge the ends of the earth and will give power to His king. He will exalt the horn of His anointed.'*
>
> 1 Samuel 2:1–10 BSB

It's a beautiful message of hope. And it's so fitting that a woman, and a mother, Hannah, is God's chosen instrument towards the healing of the abuse in Israel. After all, the first major abuser mentioned in Scripture is a woman.

Sarai.

And the first major enabler of her abuse is her husband, Abram.

Now, trust me, God is not impressed with either of them. Belial exercises mind control over believers so well that, when we approach the Scriptures, we fall into a baited trap. Just as so many institutions develop a mindset of protecting the reputation of abusive leaders at all costs, so we devise the same mental filters for 'heroes' of the faith. We're blind to their faults and we fail to notice God's denunciation of their behaviour.

In the middle of a covenant with Abram, God declares:

> *'Know for certain that your descendants will be **strangers** in a land that is not their own, and they will be **enslaved** and **mistreated** four hundred years. But I will judge the nation they serve as **slaves**, and afterward they will depart with many possessions. You, however, will go to your fathers in peace and be buried at a ripe old age. In the fourth generation your descendants will return here, for the iniquity of the Amorites is not yet complete.'*
>
> Genesis 15:1–16 BSB

I want to remark very briefly on several aspects of abuse in the words emphasised in bold. God's announcement is very troubling. Yet it's been normalised into our understanding of covenant so that we don't realise how odd, out-of-place and unbelievably peculiar it is. God promised Abram that his descendants would be enslaved and abused.

And what is Abram's reaction? The man who later bargained with God over the fate of Sodom and Gomorrah made no comment on this prophecy. He didn't beg God to reverse this decree on his own flesh and blood. Why did he just accept it without demur?

An ancient reader who had just encountered this fearful declaration would surely be primed to wonder what Abram had done to deserve it. Why don't we? Surely it's natural to protest instinctively and immediately.

The reason for Abram's silence is relayed almost instantly. The provocative words I emphasised in bold—***slave, mistreatment*** and ***stranger***—are repeated as soon as God finishes speaking. A significant member of Abram's household is then introduced. She is an Egyptian ***slave***; and her name means *the **stranger***.[57] She suffers sustained ***mistreatment*** at the hands of Sarai, Abram's wife. Abram does not, at any point, intervene to stop the abuse. He is negligent.

So God's words to Abram, inserted in a most unusual fashion into the covenant promises, make perfect sense. They reveal that the abuse did not start when

Hagar became pregnant. It was already serious—so serious in fact that there could be no escaping a future reaping. The maltreatment Sarai had already inflicted on her while Abram, the head of the household, stood by without intervening would have to be addressed in another generation.

The sins of the fathers are visited on the children to the third and fourth generation—and it was in the fourth generation, that of Joseph and his brothers—that abuse, slavery and mistreatment started to become prominent again.

God's declaration is as much an indictment as a prophecy. He is so absolutely opposed to abuse that He spelled out His judgment upon it for all time in the very first covenant He made with His chosen family. 'You will reap what you have sown, Abram,' He effectively said. 'You have abused the stranger and the slave, and so your descendants will suffer as strangers and slaves because of your behaviour. They will reap in multiplied measure for what you have done.'

We see here, in Abram's negligence and complicity with another's cruelty, the beginning of the long and callous history of how church hierarchies react when confronted with evidence of abuse. The tendency to do nothing to prevent further harm and to side with the perpetrator against the victim is so shockingly common as to be almost, but not quite, universal.

Imagine how different our faith institutions might be if Abram had modeled repentance rather than neglect.

Imagine how different they would be if David had modelled responsibility rather than abandonment after his daughter Tamar was violated. Imagine how different they would be if leaders of today actually realised that God did not hold these heroes guiltless.

Prayer

Lord of light and grace, Father of infinite faithfulness who shows love and kindness to all Your children, have mercy on me.

Jesus said, *'No one is good, except God alone,'* but as I read and listen to the stories of Scripture, I allow that knowledge slip under the radar of my thoughts and I see the 'heroes of faith' as good. I completely overlook what You say to them, how they reap what they sow, how the generations following them suffer for their iniquity and often repeat the sins of their ancestors.

Do *You* call them 'heroes', Lord?

I am comforted by that human label, Father, because I think to myself, 'Well, by comparison, I'm not doing so badly, all things considered.' It's a false comfort, Lord, a false refuge—because I should be looking to the 'good'. To You. I need goodness to overcome the spirit of abuse. I need Your empowerment—to usher me under the Cloud and carry me over the Cornerstone. I need Jesus. And yes, part of my heart is committed to Him. But another part, a part mostly hidden from me, is stuck in denial. It's cloaked in deceit and won't admit to its unbelief. It would rather trust in Time than confess that it doesn't truly believe the atonement of Jesus is sufficient for the healing I need. It would rather trust in Belial than confess that it doesn't truly believe the atonement of Jesus is sufficient to bring me into my calling. It would rather trust in the innate 'goodness of humanity' than confess that it doesn't truly believe the atonement of Jesus is my only defence in times of trouble.

Lord, we have met the enemy and he is us. I am fighting against myself through my complicity with Your adversaries. Lord, forgive me. Help me to see how I'm resourcing the war against myself, and to stop. I repent of my collaboration, Lord, but I need help to change because I truly have no idea of the extent of it.

Father, if the curse of the House of Eli has come into my family through honouring others more than we honour You, I ask You—through the power of the cross of Jesus—to cancel the curse. Let there be no more untimely death, no more physical or spiritual blindness. Lord, restore to us the blessings and inheritance You have always had in mind for us.

Teach us how to honour others rightly, to honour the world You have made, to honour all Your creation. Teach us how not to dishonour the fallen ones. Teach us how to honour and glorify Your name above all. Show us what honour looks like to You, Father, so that we honour and worship You in spirit and in truth.

Blessing and honour and glory and power be to You, to Your Son Jesus and to the Holy Spirit.

Forever and ever. Amen.

7
Replacing the Cornerstone

IT'S EASY TO OVERLOOK THE OBVIOUS when it comes to Jerusalem. Apart from its strategic location, it didn't have much going for it—at least initially. The water supply was abysmal. The neighbours were less than desirable and there was no removing them. They stuck like burrs to the land. Spiritually, it was a disaster zone.

In addition, it wasn't a place which was 'first' in any historical sense. Thus any claim it had to 'cornerstone status' was highly questionable.[58]

It wasn't the first place that Abraham built an altar and made a sacrifice to God in the land promised to his descendants. That was Moreh, near Shechem.

It wasn't the first place that Jacob, father of the twelve tribes, worshipped God by anointing a stone at the foot of a doorway to heaven. That was Bethel.

It wasn't the first place that Joshua, on crossing the Jordan and arriving in the Promised Land, led the people in a reaffirmation of Israel's covenant with God. That was Gilgal.

It wasn't the first city built by a Hebrew in the land God had pledged to give people of Israel. That was Beth Horon.

It wasn't first in any respect. It wasn't even the first royal seat. That was Gibeah of Benjamin, the hometown of Saul.

All in all, at the time Isaiah proclaimed God would lay a cornerstone in Zion, there wasn't a single reason to lay claim to it. And there were lots of reasons to hold back.

The city seems only to have been called 'Jerusalem' at some time during David's reign.[59] Its prior name was 'Jebus' after the Jebusites who had lived there prior to David's conquest—and who remained even afterwards.

Now the first gift God gave to Adam, after that of life itself, was the right to be a regent of names. As Adam named the animals, he acted as an image-bearer of God. We are image-bearers because we have a divine calling—we are summoned by God to do good works that will advance His kingdom. The specific calling given to each of us as individuals is embodied in our names. Both identity and destiny are linked in and through our names.

Cities, like people, have an identity and a destiny encoded in their names. The very first time the name 'Jebus'—as opposed to 'Jebusite', a resident of the city—appears in Scripture, it's mentioned in the prelude to the most horrific act of violence and abuse in all Israelite history—that of the Levite and his concubine.

Jebus, *trodden*—as in *threshing floor*—is poetically connected to Jabez, the name of the man famous for his prayer to be released from pain and granted an expansion of his territory. Jabez's birth was difficult so his mother named him *pain*. But his name also means *persecution* and *walled up*.

Neither Jebus nor Jabez means anything remotely like Jerusalem, *foundation of peace*. As we look at Jerusalem in the twenty-first century with its separation barrier wall and constant military presence, it looks like a manifestation of 'Jebus'. That ancient layer of meaning hasn't dissolved away: in fact, it seems to have pushed its way back to the surface.

The destiny attached to an old name—whether it's a person or a place—doesn't just vanish because we don't use it anymore. It's part of the foundation. It's integral to the cornerstone.

Jerusalem's cornerstone didn't change when Jebus was renamed, once David had solved the riddle of the locals who taunted him that even the blind and lame could ward him off. Nor did its cornerstone suddenly became that of the nation.

David at that point had been ruling in Hebron[60] for seven years. He captured the Jebusite fortress by climbing up a water shaft, and thereafter made it his capital—first, the City of David, and later Jerusalem. Now whether David's action was legitimate is an open question. Was he actually entitled to make it his capital, simply by right of conquest?

Jebus was located within the boundary allotment given to Benjamin. However David belonged to the tribe of Judah. Perhaps David justified the acquisition through his marriage to Michal, Saul's daughter. But, as a general rule, land was not to be ceded from one tribe to another this way.[61]

In order to possess a prime slice of hilltop real estate, David effectively moved a boundary line. Remember boundaries and the wellspring of life? Now if the dubious background of prior Jebusite ownership wasn't enough, David added to the tangled spirituality by altering God's allotment for the tribal brotherhood. It's one thing to help a neighbouring clan conquer an enemy stronghold within their territory, but it's entirely another to keep it for yourself. In the generations-long conflict between the people of Bethlehem and the people of Gibeah, this looks suspiciously like opportunism edged with abuse.[62]

All too often believers have the attitude, 'But it's David, so it *must* be okay! He was a man after God's own heart.' Now maybe David's actions aren't as bad as they look, but the optics aren't good. The people of Benjamin wouldn't have been out of line to call what he did 'theft', but they were a miniscule minority in Israel who simply didn't have the numbers to push for justice.

The more I read about David—a complex man who was startling blend of the utmost humility and staggering pride, as well as tender affection balanced by callous practicality—the more I'm unsure what *'a man after God's own heart'* actually means. I used to think it was because David kept covenant, but then I realised that wasn't always true. Then I thought it was because he repented when he sinned, but that's not always true either. Maybe it's because he was *willing* to repent—once it dawned on him he was actually in the wrong. Michael Heiser suggests that it simply means David's loyalty to Yahweh was such that he didn't worship other gods.

At one point David decided on a census of the fighting men. Joab, the commander of his army, tried to talk him out of it. Now Joab wasn't the most sensitive of men; he was ruthless and pragmatic. But even he was spiritually aware enough to realise this decree was about reliance on manpower and not on God—and therefore it was sin. It would put the entire nation in danger. Yet David overruled Joab's protests and it was nine months and twenty days before he finally reached the same conclusion: his sin would have deadly consequences. Given three options of punishment, he asks that—whatever happens—he will fall into the hands of God, not men.

A plague came and devastated Israel. As it reached Jerusalem, the Lord spoke to the destroying angel and said,

> *'Enough! Withdraw your hand!'*
>
> *The angel of the Lord was then standing at the threshing floor of Araunah the Jebusite.*
>
> *David looked up and saw the angel of the Lord standing between heaven and earth, with a drawn sword in his hand... Then David and the*

elders, clothed in sackcloth, fell facedown... While Araunah was threshing wheat, he turned and saw the angel; his four sons who were with him hid themselves. Then David approached, and ... said to him, 'Let me have the site of your threshing floor so I can build an altar to the Lord, that the plague on the people may be stopped. Sell it to me at the full price.'

...

David paid Araunah six hundred shekels of gold for the site ... He called on the Lord, and the Lord answered him with fire from heaven on the altar of burnt offering.

1 Chronicles 21:15–26 NIV

Obviously the Jebusites were still in the vicinity of Jerusalem. Araunah—this might not be a name but a ruler's title—was probably the king of the local Canaanite population. He had a threshing floor right next to the boundary of Jerusalem. Now a threshing floor was not simply a place for grain to be threshed, sifted and winnowed. In Canaanite religion it was a portal between heaven and earth, a 'thin place'—an ideal spot for divination and summoning of spirits.

Here is a complete upending of any neat theological package—the angel appeared at a pagan ritual site. Yet God set His mark in this most unexpected of all places. The site for Solomon's temple was this a defiled, polluted threshing floor.

The new cornerstone would be set here. Yes, historically it's Moriah, the mountain where Abraham was willing to sacrifice Isaac. However, in David's time it was a contact point for godlings and spirits of the Canaanite religion—a place of idolatry, necromancy and divination.

Even much later into Isaiah's era, the stench was still putrid. By then, there were covenants with Death and hell, false refuges, idol worship, lack of faith so extreme that God's chosen people dabbled in sorcery to summon the warrior dead to protect them from the Assyrians.

That picture of Jerusalem is an image of the state of our soul when we are complicit with Belial. When our ancestors have cut a covenant with Death or with hell, or with Time or with plague to protect them from itself (yes, the kind of perverted and irrational thinking that can only be explained by the mind control of Belial), that covenant doesn't end with their deaths. It flows on through the generations until someone revokes it. And there's no safe way to do that because so many curses are attached for violating it. We have to hand it over to Jesus to annul. Only through the power of His cross will those curses become void.

Isaiah has some very significant words to say about cornerstones and the spirit of abuse. It's not obvious he's linked the two but his prophecy in Isaiah 28 is once-and-future, it's now-and-not-yet. We know it's ultimately about Jesus, but the people of his era would have seen the fulfilment in their own days of the *'strange work'* Isaiah promised that God would perform. Isaiah alludes to a *'disturbing task'* involving time, and that is precisely what happens in that mysterious episode where the shadow on the king's steps moved backwards. He also references God's past actions involving weather and that too came to pass when the Assyrian armies are wiped out by objects hurtling down from the sky—either hail or meteorites.

It's taken me a very long time to reach Isaiah 28, even though I foreshadowed its importance in the first chapter. This is a message of rebuke and of hope.

> *Indeed, with mocking lips and foreign tongues, He will speak to this people to whom He has said: 'This is the place of rest, let the weary rest; this is the place of repose.' But they would not listen.*
>
> *Then the word of the Lord to them will become: 'Order on order, order on order, line on line, line on line; a little here, a little there,' so that they will go stumbling backward and will be injured, ensnared, and captured.*
>
> *Therefore hear the word of the Lord, O scoffers who rule this people in Jerusalem. For you said, 'We have made a covenant with Death; we have fashioned an agreement with Sheol. When the overwhelming scourge passes through it will not touch us, because we have made lies our refuge and falsehood our hiding place.'*

So this is what the Lord God says:

> *'See, I lay a stone in Zion, a tested stone,*
> *a precious cornerstone, a sure foundation;*
> *the one who believes will never be shaken.*
>
> *I will make justice the measuring line and righteousness the level. Hail will sweep away your refuge of lies, and water will flood your hiding place. Your covenant with Death will be dissolved, and your agreement with Sheol will not stand. When the overwhelming scourge passes through, you will be trampled by it. As often as it passes through, it will carry you away; it will sweep through morning after morning, by day and by night.'*

The understanding of this message will bring sheer terror. Indeed, the bed is too short to stretch out on, and the blanket too small to wrap around you. For the Lord will rise up as at Mount Perazim. He will rouse Himself as in the Valley of Gibeon, to do His work, His strange work, and to perform His task, His disturbing task.

So now, do not mock, or your shackles will become heavier. Indeed, I have heard from the Lord God of Hosts a decree of destruction against the whole land.

Listen and hear my voice. Pay attention and hear what I say.

Does the plowman plow for planting every day? Does he continuously loosen and harrow the soil? When he has levelled its surface, does he not sow caraway and scatter cumin? He plants wheat in rows and barley in plots, and rye within its border. For his God instructs and teaches him properly. Surely caraway is not threshed with a sledge, and the wheel of a cart is not rolled over the cumin. But caraway is beaten out with a stick, and cumin with a rod. Grain for bread must be ground, but it is not endlessly threshed. Though the wheels of the cart roll over it, the horses do not crush it.

This also comes from the Lord of Hosts, who is wonderful in counsel and excellent in wisdom.

Isaiah 28:11–29 BSB

This is an immensely rich and complex poem I suspect would take several books to scratch even the surface of, let alone do justice to its profundity and depth. The poem actually starts earlier and I recommend you read it all a number of times, even back into the previous chapter and forward into the next, to catch its nuances. You'll probably pick up a few I've missed. I've been chipping away at this poem for thirteen years, gradually realising it's not an eclectic stream-of-consciousness jumble but a brilliantly crafted exposition of what an ideal cornerstone should look like. It was a shock to realise that the name of the human being who laid this cornerstone was coded, quite transparently, several times in the Hebrew of the poem.

The central focus, the climax of the poem, speaks of the cornerstone and the inscription on it, as well as God's promise to lay it in Zion as a holy foundation. Ultimately, I believe the poem suggests that God is going to move a pre-existing cornerstone—one of the ones I mentioned at the beginning of this chapter—and replace the defiled one in Jerusalem with a restored foundation based on that pattern.

We, however, know that the Cornerstone is Jesus. But that's not what Isaiah's original audience would have understood. They wouldn't have seen the Cornerstone as a person but as a rock. They would have realised that it signified atonement, along with covering and covenant, but not that the rock was God incarnate, several centuries yet unborn.

Furthermore they would have been very surprised by the design of the cornerstone that Isaiah constantly hints God chose. Yet the prophet makes an excellent case for this choice by alluding to two extraordinary battles fought on it. And he prophesies that God will again show Himself strong against Time and Belial-backed armies, if only people would renounce their unholy alliances. A covenant with Death, he is saying, is no deterrent to the Assyrians.

Let me summarise what's in this chapter—besides the cornerstone. There are thin coverings, deadly covenants, perversions and inversions, false refuges, laughter and mockery, threshing floors, trampling, armies, time, deluges of water, justice and injustice, abuse. Not all of those things are on the surface, many of them are hidden in allusions.

Belial doesn't want us to understand this chapter—and so exerts a tremendous amount of mind control even in our own times to ensuring this doesn't happen. It's easy to spot such mind control because so many teachers quote verse 13 in an entirely perverted fashion. This is the verse, *'Order on order, order on order, line on line, line on line...',* perhaps more familiar to many of us as *'precept upon precept, precept upon precept, line upon line, line upon line.'*[63] So many preachers like to say they are building a solid foundation of Scripture for their listeners through this biblical principle. Except—it's the very antithesis of a biblical principle. I have to admit that I turn off the video, switch off the audio, or glance around discreetly to find an exit from the seminar room the moment I hear that unfinished quote. Because I know what end of the verse is.

> *'Here a little, there a little, that they may go, and fall backward, and be broken, and snared, and taken.'*

This verse is actually about how *not* to lay a foundation. Don't take a little here and a little there, don't rip anything out of context to make a case. And having said that, I'm not going to unpack Isaiah 28 because it requires far too much complicated background on the history and geography of Israel which cannot be corralled into a few pages. I'm going to refer to very significant parts of it, but let me encourage you to meditate on it and identify those elements I mentioned three paragraphs back.

Nevertheless there's a reason I've brought it up and quoted so much of the chapter above. It's because, right at the end, it slips in an entirely unexpected element found nowhere else in Scripture. Up to the point where it says, *'Listen and pay attention to what I say,'* Isaiah hasn't said anything completely unique. The same ideas are elsewhere. But then he slips in something extraordinary and wonderful.

He suggests that God has given us certain seed-bearing plants as an aid to restoring physical health after damage by trauma or abuse. At first, the agricultural details at the end of the chapter meant nothing to me: they seemed so random and haphazard. The different seeds were just one more disparate element in the chaotic jumble. But when I realised the significance of threshing floors in relation to cornerstones, and noted the seeds were all mentioned in a discussion of threshing, I reconsidered the matter and came to the conclusion there is nothing coincidental in the choice of grain and seeds Isaiah has mentioned. I think, strange as it may seem, that God has actually given us a diet plan to overcome the effects of abuse.

Unfortunately we cannot be sure of two of the five seeds. Those that can be positively identified are black cumin, wheat and barley. The other two are variously translated as caraway, dill or fennel, and then rye, spelt or emmer.

Wheat, of course, is one of the most genetically modified grains on the planet. No surprise, really. Quite apart from genetic modification being a signature element in Belial's modus operandi, would he want to leave us with such a simple and commonly available restorative from the effects of abuse? The dramatic rise of gluten intolerance is directly related to the fact much contemporary grain bears no resemblance to any naturally occurring plant.

The war that Belial is conducting against humanity is not just on the spiritual and emotional level but also on the physical level. Just as this spirit once changed our biosphere so greatly that the best cleansing option was a global flood, so it continues in its same efforts to ruin God's re-creation of our world and to savage both redeemed and unredeemed humanity.

Now Jesus, although He is the Cornerstone and although He is the Cloud and although He shows us exactly what the components of victory against the spirit of abuse are, doesn't really show us in a clear and unequivocal way how to achieve it. At least, not to my mind, not in one single straightforward sequence. However there is someone who does show us how it's done. It's someone Isaiah alludes to, without mentioning his name, in reference to the design of the ideal cornerstone. That someone is Joshua.

When Joshua faced off against the spirit of abuse, it came out fighting on several fronts. Centuries later Isaiah, in referring to the way God will annul a covenant with Death, said that:

> *He will rouse Himself as in the Valley of Gibeon,*
> *to do His work, His strange work, and to perform*
> *His task, His disturbing task.*
>
> Isaiah 28:21 BSB

Isaiah was referring to the 'unnatural' events that occurred during a battle between the Israelites and five armies. He was alluding to that unbelievable moment when:

> *Joshua said to the Lord in the presence of Israel:*
> *'Sun, stand still over Gibeon, and you, moon, over*
> *the Valley of Aijalon.'*
>
> *So the sun stood still, and the moon stopped.*
>
> Joshua 10:12-13 NIV

Joshua needed more **time** to successfully finish the battle, so he asked for the Lord to reveal Himself as Lord of Time by stopping the movement of the sun and moon. After all, that was how time was then measured. The flow of time was disrupted, just as it was in Isaiah's day during the Assyrian invasion when his prophecy came true and the shadow on the king's stair moved backwards. The Assyrians—long regarded as the cruellest of ancient civilisations—were under the yoke of the spirit of abuse. Twice in the book of Nahum the Assyrians are described as being counselled by Belial.[64]

God's actions in suspending the normal flow of time show that we cannot simply confront Belial as the spirit of abuse, we also have to oppose it as the spirit of Time.

We have to renounce our complicity with the two faces, not just one.

And furthermore in the time-disrupting events—that of Joshua and that of Isaiah's Jerusalem—there were armies to face. In Joshua's case, there were five of them. And like the rulers of Jerusalem who had a covenant with Death, he too had an ungodly covenant to deal with. His was with the Gibeonites. And that was one he couldn't get out of. That was unfortunate for him but fortunate for us. Because it shows us how to react in situations involving covenants we can't get out of.

Let's back up and examine how Joshua got himself into this predicament. There had been two victories—one at Jericho and one at Ai. The Israelites then went to Shechem to renew their covenant with God, as Moses had commanded them to do. This involved dividing the tribes and having one group stand on Mount Ebal and another on Mount Gerizim, calling out blessings and curses. Rather reminiscent of the Watchers throwing curses at each other on Mount Hermon. Down below in the valley between these mountain ridges was Shechem—here Abram had built his first altar to God, here Jacob had sunk a well and buried his household gods, here was where Joseph was about to be buried, his casket having been carted through the wilderness for forty years.

Things were going well for the Israelites. They relaxed a bit. A lot. And then Gibeonite envoys arrived. Not unlike Babylonian envoys, in a much later time, arrived at the court of Hezekiah. Both the Babylonians and the Gibeonites had a hidden agenda. Now the Gibeonites came, so they said, from a far country to make a treaty. Joshua and the Israelite leaders were suspicious, but not suspicious enough to inquire of the Lord. They made a covenant only to discover three days later they'd been duped. Was there some **mind control** being practised? Maybe. That doesn't absolve the leadership of not taking the matter to the Lord.

Once they realised the Gibeonites had deceived them, the Israelites were in serious trouble. Trapped. Caught in a **double-bind**. One way or another, they were going to be disobedient to the Lord. Either through a covenant breach or through ignoring the command to wipe out all the Canaanites. It's not apparent at this early stage that it's Belial the Israelites are facing—it could be any of the threshold guardians. Only when the Gibeonites are attacked by their erstwhile allies amongst the Canaanite kings and they send to the Israelites, begging for help, does the evidence start to emerge. Basically, the Gibeonites made a demand for defence on the basis of the threshold covenant—which they were entitled to do—but there's a twist in it. This is the enemy of Israel saying, 'Fight on our behalf.' It's a variation on the theme of **resourcing the war against yourself**.

The second element that suggests Belial is involved is the five **armies**. Interesting that, by the time heaven's armies are also involved, there are seven altogether.

> *The Lord said to Joshua, 'Do not fear them, for I have given them into your hands. Not a man of them shall stand before you.' So Joshua came upon them suddenly, having marched up all night from Gilgal.*[65] *And the Lord threw them into a panic before Israel, who struck them with a great blow at Gibeon and chased them by the way of the ascent of Beth-horon and struck them as far as Azekah and Makkedah. And as they fled before Israel, while they were going down the ascent of Beth-horon, the Lord threw down large stones from heaven on them as far as Azekah, and they died.*
>
> Joshua 10:8–11 ESV

Both the cornerstone and the cloud are mentioned in this passage, though neither are initially obvious. This very mysterious incident involves both weather and time. As we learn from the following verse the sun is in the east and the moon is in the west while this segment reveals there's a storm overhead—of either hailstones or meteorites. Hailstones implies rainclouds and meteorites implies aurora-like ionisation trails, so either way there's a thin covering. (Meteor, by the way, derives from the Greek for *things in heaven above*, which is why we can also have meteors from *space*, and also meteorology, being the study of the *atmosphere*, clouds and weather.)

The cornerstone is more elusive. It's alluded to in the repeated reference to Beth Horon, an obscure town in Ephraim close to the border with the territory of

Benjamin. It was the very first city constructed by a descendent of Abraham in the land God promised him as an inheritance. And it was built long before the time of Joshua, in fact centuries previously, by no less than the granddaughter of Joseph.

> *Ephraim had a daughter named Sheerah. She built the towns of Lower and Upper Beth-horon and Uzzen-sheerah.*
>
> 1 Chronicles 7:24 NLT

Ephraim was Joseph's younger son. We know absolutely nothing about his daughter Sheerah except:

- she was born after Ephraim lost his family in a revenge raid when his sons decided to rustle some cattle
- she had a brother named Beriah, and
- she built two or three cities, depending on whether we count Lower and Upper Beth Horon as one or two towns.

Because Beth Horon was a 'first', it genuinely has a claim to cornerstone status. Now Beth Horon doesn't just feature in the battle between Joshua and the five armies; it also features in the battle of Mount Perazim—a conflict between David and the Philistines who, from the extremely poetic description of what happened, seemed to have had one flank of their attack force smashed by an inland tsunami. The other flank fled up the ascent of Beth Horon where, like the armies in the time of Joshua, they were soundly defeated.

Another significant battle was also won here, but is not mentioned by Isaiah: the battle started by Jonathan and his armour-bearer against the Philistines at Michmash. An earthquake came to Jonathan's aid and rattled the already confused enemy, scattering them and sending them fleeing along the road to Beth Horon where they were finally defeated.

The Ascent of Beth Horon was always associated in Hebrew history with the final defeat of Israel's enemies after supernatural intervention by God. It continued that association long after the time of Isaiah when the Maccabees won a decisive battle there, as did the rebel Jewish forces in the year 66 at the start of the war with Rome.

What was it about Beth Horon that God continued, time after time, century after century, to show up as the Lord of Hosts, the Commander of the Armies of Heaven, and defend His people with supernatural signs and wonders? I have to suspect it was because Sheerah created a threshold covenant in the land itself. The symbolism of a covenant ceremony is about two halves becoming one. Her two-in-one town was named Beth Horon. The one at the top was Upper and the one at the bottom of the hill was Lower but they both had the same name: it was an image of covenant inscribed into the landscape itself. With remarkable forethought for what she was doing, Sheerah cut a covenant between her communities and the God of Abraham, Isaac, Jacob and Joseph. She didn't know Him as Yahweh but she still sought Him as covenant defender. And her covenant outlived her—because that's what covenants do.

I don't have any doubt that Isaiah immensely admired Sheerah's handiwork—he encoded her name through puns, rhymes and wordplay at least five times into the poem that makes up Isaiah 28. And, I suspect, he was inspired to name his son, Shear-Jashub, after her. They are the only two people mentioned in Scripture whose names contain the element 'sheer-', *remnant*.

Such a wondrous cornerstone—one where divine covenantal defence is assured—was exactly what Jerusalem needed in the time of Isaiah. And it was exactly what it didn't have. But then, remarkably, Isaiah prophesied that God would lay a cornerstone in Zion that had all the qualities of the covenantal space between Sheerah's cities. A place where Time held no sway, where the angel hosts would fight with you against a fivefold enemy, where a cloud canopy would be your covering above and a cornerstone laid by the Ancient of Days Himself be your covering beneath, and His glory would be your rearguard and He would shake your enemies with earthquakes or wash them away in a torrent.[66]

In short order, after Isaiah prophesied this, time actually took several backward steps in Jerusalem:

> *This is the Lord's sign to you... 'I will make the shadow cast by the sun go back the ten steps it has gone down on the stairway of Ahaz.' So the sunlight went back the ten steps it had gone down.*
>
> Isaiah 38:7–8 NIV

Furthermore, angel hosts wiped out the Assyrian army at the approaches to the city:

> *That night the angel of the Lord went out and put to death a hundred and eighty-five thousand in the Assyrian camp. When the people got up the next morning—there were all the dead bodies!*
>
> Isaiah 37:36 NIV

What does all this tell us about abusers on our doorstep?

It tells us this. We need to position ourselves so that we can be assured of the divine defence that comes from having Jesus of Nazareth as our covenant defender.

- ✘ That requires us to renounce our false refuges and our covenants with Death and with hell.
- ✘ We need to stop mocking God.
- ✘ We need to cease using sorcery by manipulating the creative power of His Word or the redemptive power of the blood of Jesus to achieve our desires.
- ✘ We may still have double-binds operating but we need to negotiate them as best we can, honouring God as best we can.
- ✓ We need the right Cornerstone.
- ✓ We need the right Cloud covering.

✓ We need to call on God as the Lord of Time.
✓ We need to call on God as Lord of Hosts.

Until we've dealt with the curses and choices attached to the first four issues, we will not be able to receive the last four blessings.

To start this process, it's always appropriate to begin with **false refuges**—those habits we use to comfort ourselves when we are disappointed with God. You think you've never been disappointed with God? Take a further step back then, behind the starting line, and pray about the mind control you're experiencing. Consult the book on false refuges—*Hidden in the Cleft*.

Only when you've been tested and

✓ passed the temptation to flee to one of your false refuges
✓ after having repented of using them as your consolation in times of trouble

are you ready to **renounce the ungodly covenants** in your life. This may take time: God has appointed a season for you to show yourself faithful to Him and you'll need His strength to pass through it without defaulting to your coping mechanism. See the appendices in *God's Pottery: The Sea of Names and the Pierced Inheritance*.

Mockery: simply inquire of God how you dishonour Him and others. And repent. Keep going back and back to Him, however many times it takes—seventy times seven per day, if necessary—and ask Him for help in getting it right.

Magic and sorcery: if you have complicity with either Belial or Kronos, this is a given. Quite likely, you are not aware you have crossed a line. And that's part of the point of their mind control.

Double-binds: this can lead to what is called 'betrayal blindness', a condition that reinforces the mind control. Jennifer Freyd coined this phrase to describe what happens when someone is abused and betrayed by a person they both trust and depend on. Caught in a 'bind between two needs'—to stop the abuse and also to preserve the relationship—they become blind to truth. It is too risky to acknowledge.

Covering: covenants are about covering. When Isaiah pointed out that the bed is too short and the blanket too narrow, he was saying that, if we hop into bed with an unholy spirit, then its covenantal defence will be a much thinner covering than we want. There's such a thing as *too* thin. Full covering, the kind that comes from passing over a cornerstone, is about belief in the atonement. And if you really believed in that, you wouldn't have a problem with any of the threshold spirits. Again, the book in the series that looks at unbelief in the atonement is *Hidden in the Cleft*.

By now, you may be thinking: but I wanted an answer *now*. All these things will take *time*. You're right. You see, as I mentioned, the Fruit of the Spirit that overcomes abuse is 'chesed', *goodness, kindness, faithfulness*. Know what? The only way we can demonstrate faithfulness is through constant fidelity *over time*.

You might now be thinking: this feels much more like *doing* time than *redeeming* time. And indeed without the Lord's help—the Lord who is the redeemer of wasted time—we will default back into our preferred system of abuse. Doing time is a prison sentence and that's precisely what Belial wants for us—hard labour with no opportunity for parole, working on his behalf to dig our own grave, paying him for the privilege of destroying our planet.

On the other hand, Jesus wants to give us back time. And freedom and rest. Not to mention joy. Every Sukkot—every Feast of Tabernacles when rest, joy and 'cloud'-watching were *commanded*—He showed us some aspect of what it means to take back the stewardship of earth.

So let us take up the 'yiredu', *dominion*, God gave us through honour for Him and respect for His creation. Let us accept the water libation God has given us in baptism by renewing those vows that bind us to Him and by daily responding to the call of Jesus: *'Come, come to the waters.'*

Amen and amen.

Prayer

The following declaration and prayer is a variation on a centuries-old liturgy for the Eastertide renewal of baptismal promises. Throughout Scripture God calls people to reaffirm their covenant with Him; in fact, the Israelites were instructed that, on entering the Promised Land, they were to go to Shechem and stand in two groups, one on Mount Ebal and one on Mount Gerezim, there to recite the blessings and curses of the divine covenant on one another. This prayer follows that understanding of a need to rededicate ourselves to God.

Heavenly Father, I ask You to empower my words in the name of Your beloved Son, the Lord Jesus Christ, who ascended the Mount of Assembly to rebuke the evil one and raise a standard for His own government. I ask that the Holy Spirit seal and authorise my words and record them in Your scroll of days:

I renounce the satan. I renounce Belial. I renounce Kronos. I renounce the evil one under whatever name he hides. I renounce the enemy of my soul.

I renounce all his works: matters of abuse, matters of time, matters of armies, matters of transgression of 'kinds'. I renounce all his empty promises. I renounce every covenant, pledge, vow and agreement that binds me into oneness with him, his servants, his allies or his children. I renounce any belief in Time as a healer or in my own ability to endure until the abuse ends.

I repent of, and turn away from, the enticements of the evil one, and I ask Jesus to cover me by His blood so that sin may have no mastery over me. I repent of my false refuges, my covenants with Death, with Hell, with Time and with any of the faces of Abuse. I repent of any involvement, knowing or unknowing, in a water-pouring ceremony that not only sends out an invitation to the Watchers but counterfeits baptism.

I ask You to carry me over the Cornerstone into the life under the Cloud where I can rest in the true and joyful freedom of the redeemed children of God.

I declare that I believe in God, the Father Almighty, Creator of heaven and earth. I further believe in Jesus Christ, His only Son, our Lord, who was born by consent of Mary to the overshadowing of the Holy Spirit, who lived in Nazareth of Galilee, who suffered death on a cross for the atonement of the sins of the world, who was buried in Jerusalem, who rose again after three days from the dead and who is seated in glory at the right hand of the Father. I also believe in the Holy Spirit, as well as the true and holy and universal church known to God, the communion of saints, the cloud of witnesses. I believe in the forgiveness of sins, the resurrection of the body, and life everlasting.

I renew my acceptance to Jesus' invitation to be born of water and the Spirit and to become His Bride. I enter His wounds by grace through faith and I ask to be hidden in His side, there protected from the assaults of the evil one.

Lastly, I ask Almighty God, Yahweh Sabaoth, the Lord of Hosts who is Father of Jesus Christ, the Lord of Time and the Redeemer of wasted time, to keep me by His grace, forevermore, within the eternal NOW of the presence of Immanuel, *God with us*. Blessing and honour, glory and power, be to His name.

Amen

Appendix 1
Summary

THE SPIRIT OF ABUSE GOES by several names. The main ones noted in this book are Belial, Kronos and the Janissary spirit.

Belial is mentioned 28 times in Scripture, once only in Greek and 27 times in Hebrew. Paul's use of the word makes it clear that it is a spiritual entity opposed to Christ, not simply an abstract quality of *worthlessness* or *wickedness*. In the religious writings of the early Christian era, Belial was one of the names for the leader of the Watchers who descended to Mount Hermon in order to mate with human women. This event is briefly summarised at the beginning of Genesis 6. The Book of 1 Enoch, a highly regarded prophecy of this era which was quoted in the epistle of Jude and referenced in Peter's writings, describes the rebellion of the Watchers in greater detail.

They had hybrid angel-human children, the *nephilim*, who were giants. The children of the *nephilim* were *gibborim*, the mighty heroes of old. These offspring were destroyed in the flood, but their spirits survived to become demons, according to the Jewish understanding of the origin of demons in the time of Jesus.

The Watchers themselves were imprisoned in Tartarus—as were the titans, the *giants*, of Greek mythology. Kronos (or Chronos or Saturn), the elder-god known as 'Father Time', was a titan. He castrated and deposed his father. He then went on to be a child-killer who devoured all his offspring so he would be safe from the same kind of fate he inflicted on his father. He thereby drove the last child, Zeus, to overthrow him. The word, 'titan', refers to *overstepping boundaries*.

Belial transgressed species-boundaries and spatial-boundaries when it descended to earth. It continues to tempt us to transgress boundaries, particularly in regard to sexuality, genetics and time—which, ultimately, includes seasons and weather. The first temptation of Jesus involved an enticement to transgress the order of 'kinds'. Because trauma has an effect on genetic structure, building a temporary 'scaffold' on DNA that lasts three or four generations, it is possible one use of abuse is to access our DNA profiles.

Belial uses group mind control to blame-shift and misdirect. It wants to keep us from approaching Jesus to redeem our wasted time, to fix the core wounding in our cornerstone and to replace the fake covering cloud with His canopy of glory. It wants to keep our inheritance and even the knowledge of our inheritance—the right to steward and govern the earth—from us. It wants to steal our healing and deny us redemption.

Belial was a throne guardian, one of the cherubim or seraphim, an official of the royal court of heaven who was closest to the Lord. It is likely the Watchers were cherubim—multi-faced, many-eyed, eternally wakeful. Not all Watchers rebelled against the Lord but those that did had an intimate knowledge of God's plan of salvation for humanity. They knew sufficient detail to try to pre-empt and circumvent God's redemptive purposes. It cannot be coincidental that the action of the fallen Watchers in appropriating 'good' human women to bear demi-gods foreshadows and counterfeits the work of the Holy Spirit in overshadowing the virgin Mary. Nor can it be coincidence that possession by demons, the departed spirits of these angelic-human hybrid demi-gods who were drowned in the flood, is a counterfeit of the indwelling of the Holy Spirit. Nor can it be coincidence that, of all the threshold spirits, Belial is the only one described as having a human family—both 'sons' and 'daughters' of Belial are attested—when the entire history of God's interaction with the people of the world reveals His intention to build and maintain a family. He chose one man, covenanted and connected and reconnected with his lineage in order to eventually redeem a family from every tribe and tongue.

The throne guardians who left their positions, their 'first estate' as Jude put it, and became fallen Watchers not only tried to anticipate God's timing and beat Him to the punch, they tried to use their own flawed version of His perfect plans. Here we see the activity of Kronos—in a timing that is out of time.

Unless we understand who our enemy is, we will not see our own complicity with it. We may think we are the abused, not the abuser. However, until we realise that Kronos, the child-slayer who wants to eat the future as well as consume the past, is one of the faces of abuse, we will not recognise our collaboration with this spirit. And unless we see the 'Janissary spirit' as yet another persona of this spirit of abuse, we won't notice how we are resourcing the war against ourselves and paying it to engineer our own destruction.

Prior to being able to tackle the spirit of abuse, we have to be positioned correctly: we need the Cornerstone beneath us and the Cloud above us. Without an immaculate Cornerstone and a tabernacling Cloud, it's pointless to start. Defeat is certain. If we rely on the cracked cornerstone we were born with and the contrail lattice of fake cloud that Belial offers as our covering, the battle is over before it's begun. We can ask for our cornerstone to be replaced, as Isaiah indicated was possible. Thus we should ask for Jesus to be our replacement threshold stone—but as Isaiah also indicates, this cannot be done until we have repented of our false refuges and renounced our ungodly covenants. We have to cease supplying the enemy with the armaments needed to conduct the war against us.

Because Belial is also a spirit of armies, as well as time, we need the true Lord of Armies and the true Lord of Time to battle on our behalf. When we find the warbands of Belial deployed against us, we need to take our stand in the covenant space above the Cornerstone and under the Cloud and call on God as the Redeemer of Time and also as Yahweh Sabaoth, the Lord of Hosts. We need to ask Him to show Himself strong under those names.

Two Scriptural examples where God simultaneously shows Himself as the Lord of Time and the Lord of Hosts are

- the battle on the Ascent of Beth Horon where Joshua asks the sun and moon to stand still
- the angelic destruction of the Assyrian army during the days of Hezekiah's illness when the shadow of the sun moved back along the stairwell

Jesus relentlessly opposed Belial as well as its alter-ego, Beelzebul. His references to the Living Water during the Feast of Sukkot give us direction for the healing of trauma. His transfiguration during the Feast of Sukkot is a fulfillment of the prophecy of Psalm 82 and the announcement of His takeover of the government of the nations. After the Tower of Babel, God had distributed the nations between seventy angel-shepherds, while reserving Israel for Himself. These principalities became corrupt, unjust and negligent over time, and God decreed their fall to mortality and death. Their abusive style mirrors the violence and depravity of Belial.

The couplet of 'appointed days'—the fast of Yom Kippur followed six days later by the Feast of Sukkot—symbolise two covenants and their coverings, the Cornerstone and the Cloud.

To be able to overcome Belial, the following are necessary as preparation ***beforehand***:

- renunciation of known false refuges and tests for overcoming
- renunciation of covenants with Death and with hell
- maturing of goodness, kindness and faithfulness as a Fruit of the Spirit
- new cornerstone with new inscription
- Cloud covering of glory and honour
- the kiss of God as armour

There's a natural season of time before it is evident that a renunciation of a covenant with Death is effective—a season long enough that faithfulness can indeed mature if we are willing to keep hold of Jesus.

Scriptural references:

- Isaiah 28 and 2 Kings 2:19–20
- Joshua 9–10

Scripture References to Belial:

1. Deuteronomy 13:13 — the law concerning worship of Belial
2. Deuteronomy 15:9 — Belial's influence leads to cruelty rather than compassion
3. Judges 19:22 — Sons of Belial attack the Levite, Jonathan, and his concubine in Gibeah
4. Judges 20:13 — The tribe of Benjamin is called to deliver up the sons of Belial in their midst
5. 1 Samuel 1:16 — Hannah insists she is not a daughter of Belial
6. 1 Samuel 2:12 — The sons of Eli the priest are described as sons of Belial
7. 1 Samuel 10:27 — Some sons of Belial treat Saul, the new king, with dishonour
8. 1 Samuel 25:17 — Abigail's husband, Nabal, is described as a son of Belial by one of his servants
9. 1 Samuel 25:25 — Abigail describes her husband, Nabal, as a son of Belial
10. 1 Samuel 30:22 — Sons of Belial amongst David's men refuse to share with their companions
11. 2 Samuel 16:7 — Shimei curses David as a 'man of Belial'
12. 2 Samuel 20:1 — Sheba rebels against David and is described as a 'man of Belial'
13. 2 Samuel 22:5 — David's song of praise describes Belial as 'torrents'

14. 2 Samuel 23:6 — David's very last words advise complete separation from sons of Belial
15. 1 Kings 21:10 — Jezebel asks for two sons of Belial to accuse Naboth of blasphemy
16. 1 Kings 21:13 — Two sons of Belial lie in public about Naboth
17. 1 Kings 21:13 — Two sons of Belial cause Naboth's death
18. 2 Chronicles 13:7 — Sons of Belial oppose Rehoboam, son of Solomon
19. Job 34:18 — It's not honouring to call a king 'a son of Belial'
20. Psalm 18:4 — Belial is described as 'torrents'
21. Psalm 41:8 — David's enemies speak of a disease from Belial afflicting him
22. Psalm 101:3 — David says he will not set any word of Belial before his eyes
23. Proverbs 6:12 — People influenced by Belial speak perversely
24. Proverbs 16:27 — People influenced by Belial spread evil talk
25. Proverbs 19:28 — Witnesses influenced by Belial pervert justice
26. Nahum 1:11 — The Assyrians are counselled by Belial
27. Nahum 1:15 — Belial will be completely destroyed
28. 2 Corinthians 6:15 — What harmony can there be between Christ and Belial?

Appendix 2

Summary of Belial's Main Tactics

- cracking your cornerstone
- group mind control
- double-bind manipulation
- blame-shifting
- denying, deflecting and defaming (or dismissing, distorting, distracting and dismaying)
- inversion of symbols, particularly religious emblems so they no longer offer comfort but trigger panic
- perversion and reversal of the common or accepted meaning of words
- depraved behaviour and cruelty
- reversing the victim and the perpetrator
- insisting on grace for the abuser at the expense of the victims
- gaslighting in such a way that both victims and observers question their perception of reality

- persuading us to resource the war against ourselves by arming and financing our enemies
- transgression of forbidden boundaries
- spell-binding and drugs ('pharmakeia', *sorcery*)
- army mentality that darkens the minds of children so they see their parents as the enemy
- time-wasting, reliance on time passing or time manipulation
- honouring others more than we honour God
- faking the covering Cloud

Appendix 3
Types of Complicity

WITHOUT DOUBT, THE HARDEST ISSUE to come to terms with is our own complicity with Belial. I'm not talking about controllers and abusers here who have an obvious alliance with this spirit. I'm talking about those of us who think we're standing against it, while in fact we are not.

You might have noticed that in this book, I haven't used the cliché, 'You're not a victim, you're a victor.' Partly because, as I've learned, it's so often a way of closing down a story of suffering and partly because, at best, it's a partial truth. Sometimes we need to tell our story—again and again—because we're still processing the ways in which we unknowingly collaborated with the enemy. We don't gain victory through complicity. And there are many ways Belial can assert legal rights in our lives, other than the usual lack of forgiveness and lack of repentance.

Some of the more subtle ways are outlined in the following.

The implied contract

In the spiritual world, as in the marketing world, 'maybe' means *yes*, and 'no' means *not yet*. This is why I use the term 'renounce' with the sense of *never again* in so many prayers. When we observe abuse and remain silent, we are effectively consenting to it and thus aligning ourselves with Belial.

Language deconstruction

Quite often, however, we are tricked by language used in deceptive ways. This is quite different to the ambiguity that is a hallmark of the spirit of Python. If you can discern a possible double meaning and query it, a person influenced by Python won't lie to you. However when you question a follower of Belial, the clarifications are not merely false, they attach a meaning to the words that is a complete inversion of any commonly accepted definition. That is, if you get any clarification at all. Belial doesn't want to dialogue—at least it doesn't want to once it's in a position of power—so it creates an impassable communication barrier and refuses to engage.

As an example of inversion, take the African proverb: *it takes a village to raise a child*. A follower of Belial would suggest this means children should be taken from their parents so that the state, as a representative of the global village, can raise them. Or take the word 'diversity', which now all too often means what was once understood by 'perversity', when its older nuance was *grace*. Or the word 'inclusion' which is no longer an all-encompassing embrace but now means 'excluding those with whom we disagree'.

Those last two are fairly obvious, but what about this one? A police officer has stopped you for a possible traffic infringement and asks you, 'Do you understand?' Maybe he's asking you if you comprehend what he's said, but maybe he's using it in the technical sense, 'Do you stand under?' and in that case, you'd definitely be agreeing with an implied contract regarding his authority. Best to always answer: 'I don't know. I heard your question but I don't know.'

When you don't know that another person is using deconstructed language and is not trying to communicate with you but control you, then it's all too easy to create a double-bind for yourself. Belial, you need to remember, does not want reconciliation but separation. It would prefer blind submission and control but, if you're going to keep asking for clarification, it wants you out.

It feels horrific to be excluded and marginalised but, in fact, God wants you to *'come out and be separate.'*

The Language of Trauma

This is about the words we ourselves use, not the language used against us. Unresolved trauma and abuse causes us to feel stuck in the past, always rehearsing in our minds and in our talk the same old same old story of how we were betrayed. We're always using the past tense, instead of the present tense. Kronos, the elder-god of time who was chained up to stop him eating the future as well as the past, is in fact oppressing us to such a degree we allow him to consume our present.

We can get mired in grief for our own losses, including that of youth and time. And so instead of looking to Jesus to redeem the time, we keep any covenant or even implied agreement with Kronos intact by our behaviour and beliefs.

Remember this: God turned back the shadow on the stairs to show Hezekiah he would be given fifteen more years of life. That did not mean Hezekiah used that time wisely; he didn't. When Jesus brings that miracle of restored and redeemed time into our lives, we have to make the choice to use it for His glory—or worse may befall our generations because we start to take God for granted.

Vows

Have you ever said to yourself, 'I am worthless'?

Tell God right now you're sorry for identifying yourself with Belial. Since one translation of the name, Belial, is *worthless*, this is effectively saying, 'I am Belial.'

No, you're not. You are not Belial, you are not worthless, you are not nothing. Jesus died because you are so precious to God that He was willing to give His life for you. You might have made terrible mistakes, you might have committed the blackest darkest vilest sin, but God still wants you to be part of His family. He wants you to *renounce*, to say a forever 'no' to any vows that keep you chained up in a double-bind so you don't feel you can leave Belial's 'family'. Simply tell God you want out and ask Him to bring it about. The time for that to occur will depending on how many false refuges and covenants you have.

Alcohol

Totally obvious, isn't it? Alcohol and abuse are linked. There's the mockery component all too often present as well. I'm not going to say too much on this because other books say it infinitely better.

But I want to note two things that they are likely to miss:

Isaiah 28 begins with a picture of drunkenness and mockery, which may in fact be associated with a 'marzeah' ceremony—an ancient ritual on behalf of the dead.

During the Middle Ages, a covenant was sealed with a 'beverage'. Nowadays beverage is simply regarded as a *drink*, but note that it's generally tacked to an intoxicating liquor as in 'alcoholic beverage'. Centuries back, 'beverage' was more about covenant than the drink itself.

Alcoholic abuse that has, as its hidden motivation, a soul tie to the dead or an ancestral covenant requires a renunciation and a severing of the soul tie or the covenant.

Pornography

A form of mind control so fierce, so alluring that, even recognising its power over us, we generally don't want to be free of it. We pay for our own downfall into depravity. The very word 'pornography' goes back in meaning to a *worship of idols*—it's therefore a false refuge, a comfort, a substitute for God.

Pornography encourages ever greater level of deviance—boundary-transgression—because, once the mind normalises coercion and rape, it no longer experiences a thrill. More novelty and brutality are needed to produce the same effect—and so the 'image-bearers' of God become commodities to be visually consumed. Vulnerable women and children, in particular, are exploited and trafficked for the sexual gratification of the viewer.

Believers, particularly those of younger age groups, are enmeshed as Belial's prey in this struggle. Real-life relationships are debased as the trapped strive against an age-old beguilement and find themselves in a double-bind trying to get out—if, of course, they decide they actually do want to get out. No flesh-and-blood man or woman can ever compare with the enthrallment of a perfect fantasy liaison where every sexual taste, even the bestial, is extravagantly fulfilled. And, of course, where 'no' really means 'yes'.

Abortion

Let us name the hidden, not so it can be glorified, but that it may be healed.

Abortion is loss of the future—not just for baby, but for the parents and others involved in the decision. Many grandparents also experience grief and loss. Siblings, unconsciously, try to take on more than one destiny to fulfil the calling of the family.

Abortion has been in existence since at least the era when the Israelites were slaves in Egypt. The Pharaoh, to limit the Hebrew population, decreed all newborn boys be killed. Here we have an early example of eugenics.

> *'He was an abusive king who exploited our people with his smooth talk. With cruelty, he forced our ancestors to give up their little boys as he committed infanticide.'*
>
> Acts 7:19 TPT

Brian Simmons states that, in Aramaic, this can also be translated: *'forced them to abort their children.'*

Why didn't the Israelites rise up in rebellion as Pharaoh feared? Were they enslaved by the trauma as much as they were by the Egyptians? The relatively modern sciencé of epigenetics tells us that trauma can have a transient effect on genes which lasts three or four generations. Mark Wolynn writes of the descendants of Holocaust survivors who, while being shielded from the past and never having heard their parent's or grandparent's stories, nevertheless experience 'inherited trauma'. Hitler wanted to abort an entire race of people; and it is no coincidence that the founder of Planned Parenthood also had a racial and eugenics agenda.

Infants and children in the womb experience pain. Why did we ever think otherwise? 'It is becoming increasingly clear that experiences of pain are "remembered" by the developing nervous system, impacting the entire life of the individual. These findings should focus the attention of clinicians on the long-term impact of early painful experiences, and highlight the urgent need for developing long term strategies for the development of neonatal and foetal pain.'[67]

When a prior abortion or termination—sometimes even a miscarriage—takes place in the womb, subsequent babies pick up on the spirit pervading their 'safe place' of nurture. To them the womb feels like a 'house of death' and can have a profound effect. Like the leaders in Jerusalem taking out a covenant with Death in order to feel safe against the Assyrian invasion, the spirit of an unborn child can ally itself with Death to feel safe in a frightening place.

Mother Teresa stated, 'The so-called right to abortion has pitted mothers against their children and women against men. It has sown violence and discord at the heart of the most intimate of human relationships. It has aggravated the derogation from the nature of father's role in an increasingly fatherless society. It has portrayed the greatest of gifts—a child—as a competitor, an intrusion and an inconvenience. It has nominally accorded mothers unfettered dominion over the dependent lives of their physically dependent sons and daughters. And, in granting this unconscionable power, it has exposed many women to unjust and selfish demands from their husbands or other sexual partners.'[68]

Psychiatrist Keith Ablow says he has 'listened to dozens of men express lingering, sometimes intense, pain over abortions that proceeded either without their consent, or without their having spoken up about their desires to bring their children to term and parent them.'[69]

Although abortion is said to alleviate child abuse, neglect studies have shown that child abuse has risen with the legalisation of abortion. We introduce a disdain for life with societal acceptance of abortion, especially life of the youngest and most elderly or those who are not perceived as 'as they should be'. This is dangerous for all of humanity, particularly the most vulnerable.

Self-rejection is the byproduct of a failed abortion on the surviving child—though, there are fewer surviving children now because of medical infanticide. The spirit of a child carries this burden through life: *if my mother, the nurturer of my life, can choose to murder me, then who am I to think I may be worthy of a place in life? Who am I to expect I am of value?*

Belial, opportunistic as every unholy spirit is, can use these questions about being *worthless* to deepen the alliance with itself. We can become unthinkingly loyal to the one trying to destroy us.

If a baby survives the trauma of a failed abortion and is not welcomed at birth, the sense of rejection, abandonment and isolation will inevitably lead to a belief system revolving around a need to disappear, to be silent and not seen or heard or acknowledged, to not have needs. Ultimately may come the decision to not exist. Throughout life, an inexplicable sense of being stolen from, possibly in all areas, may be a torment. Disconnection between heart and head is to be expected.

The anguished cry throughout life is: 'I am innocent.' However, if there are places in the heart where there is agreement with Belial or Kronos, that is not entirely true. We may have come into alignment with the covenants of previous generations. We therefore defile others through a 'bitter root expectancy'—the belief that others will reject, abandon and cast us aside, a belief so intense in some cases that we actually we set up the conditions for it to happen. Perversely, Belial has convinced us that 'safety' is in isolation and neglect, and so we push and push others until they walk out on us. We therefore need to recognise our own sinful reactions and behaviours and stop contributing to our own separation from life.

Another contributor to isolation is in not being 'chosen' for love: very specifically not being chosen at all. In fact, quite the opposite, being 'chosen' for destruction. The unborn child's spirit draws back from welcoming life to accommodating an alliance with Death. The child's belief system becomes grounded in lies: *no right to live and no right to belong.* Moreover, the spirit develops a deep sense of no security, no love and no safe place. Hiding is the best option. The tension between *being* and *not being dead* creates a withdrawal from life through fear, anxiety, confusion, anger, hatred, shame, hatred of mother and father and perhaps a sense of guilt in surviving, living as well.

Some children take on the belief they are burdens, not just mistakes. They take refuge in compliancy. Others may be very angry and demand their place in life and family. Some try to make a statement by self-destructive behaviour, or by shaming their parents and family as a form of backlash. All of these are rooted in a 'guilt' for existing.

Belial—and Moloch too—convinces us that we need to sacrifice our children for prosperity. Sometimes he'll even manage to convince believers that it's for ministry! Prosperity—'shalom', *peace, well-being, welfare, soundness, completeness, security, safety*—is however the very thing that all too many people surrender through abortion. Although many mothers feel initial relief after an abortion, it generally fades into long-term depression. This is often, once again, the 'stuckness' of grief. And also, once again, we resource the war against ourselves.

Abortion is a blood sacrifice not only of our children, but of our blessing in time to come. It is a sacrifice to self as well as to Kronos. We allow him access to our destiny, spoiling the future and hope God has for us. Instead of ancient sacrifices to godlings of production, fertility, weather, and comfort, today's pet godlings are prosperity, education, career, convenience, choice, affluence and lifestyle choices. Our love of money and entertainment hardens our hearts to the cry and needs of the single mums, the rape victims, the disabled and those for whom it is just plain difficult to manage a baby—or another baby. It's a mistake to believe people do not care when they may really be saying, 'I am fearful!'

Spiritually, abortion may open the mother's door to fear of exposure, guilt, shame, fear, grief and loss, pain, condemnation and self-condemnation, trauma, judgment, running to escape the trauma, terror, violence (towards the baby), hatred of self and others who did not support and perhaps mental illness and even suicide attempts. According to the *British Medical Journal* women with a history of abortion are 81% more likely to face mental health issues.[70] We cannot undo our past choices just as we cannot unscramble an egg, but we have to be willing to ask for the chains of shame to be unlocked. One minister in a major inner-city church questioned why he has not been approached by unmarried women who have shared the story of their pregnancies or the seeking of an abortion.[71] Like the spirit of a child survivor of a failed abortion needing to hide, the spirit of the mother in a successful abortion all too often feels the need to hide as well.

Frank Pavone writes, 'The other phenomenon at work is denial—a denial fuelled by pain and sustained by fear. Those who participate in an abortion decision—and there are more each day—are rarely eager to get involved in an effort to expose the process they just went through. In fact, the wound of abortion is severe enough that many who went through it don't even want to hear the word *abortion*, let alone to explore its ramifications. This indicates why the mission of healing is so urgent. The more women who have had abortions we help heal, the more they will be able to face abortion and therefore fight it... There are an even larger number of people, however, whose pain over abortion comes not from the direct personal involvement but from a failure to act.'[72]

In healing from abortion we are handing to Jesus the ashes of our lives. These ashes are our own sinful reactions to our belief system, and they have been ruling us. Theirs is the dominion, not ours. The vows and judgments we've believed about ourselves and life need to be toppled so that we can accept the love of Jesus, walk in His shalom—true prosperity and wholeness—and become a blessing to others.

We need to 'see' our lost child as a person with a spirit and a name. Seek prayer ministry with a person who can bring you safely into the presence of God in His throneroom so you can ask your heavenly Father what name He had chosen for your aborted baby. Some mothers and fathers find it helpful to write a letter asking forgiveness, talking of a newfound love for the little one, and then burying it somewhere 'special'.

One of the Hebrew words for destiny is 'meni', *award*, referring to a pagan god of fate. The word for *good fortune* is 'gad', which also happens to be a word for an *army troop*. In pursuing luck and destiny, we can all too often be chasing down Belial, that spirit of abuse and armies. We can be running towards warfare, not away from it. Isaiah, once again, explains it all:

> *But as for you who forsake the Lord,*
> *and forget My holy mountain,*
> *who spread a table for Fortune,*
> *and fill bowls with mixed wine for Destiny,*
> *I will destine you for the sword,*
> *and all of you will fall in the slaughter*
> *for I called, but you did not answer;*
> *I spoke, but you did not listen.*
> *You did evil in My sight*
> *and chose that which displeases Me.*
>
> Isaiah 65:11–12 NIV

Who would want such a future? We have a choice to step into all the Lord God has assigned for us, His destiny—the one He has implanted within our names—or we can choose to go another way in our life. Our destiny in God includes the fulfillment of all we are called to be, the satisfaction of seeing our dreams take shape, the joy of resting in Him. *'Come out from them and be separate'* becomes the clarion cry to cast off our complicity with the powers of darkness and to walk in the fullness and freedom Jesus offers.

Appendix 4
'Dat Ribber in Egypt'

Sometimes one of my parents would say to the other: 'What's wrong?'

And the answer would be: 'Dat ribber in Egypt.'

It was a pun, although the issue they were facing was always serious. 'Dat ribber in Egypt' was 'that river in Egypt', the Nile: 'da Nile', *denial.*

Complicity with Belial includes denial. However when it comes to tackling denial in relation to abuse, there are different upstream flows to be considered. It's important to take a look at those inlets of motivation to know whether it's actually worth putting in the effort to try to counter the denial.

The first kind, which has been mentioned previously, is used by the abuser. It's part of the lies and gaslighting. It's integral to the *deny-deflect-defame* strategy. It's a waste of time trying to penetrate the denial structure an abuser builds. Every dent you make, every falsehood you expose, will only reassure the abusers—and their friends—that you are on the side of the 'real' perpetrator.

The second kind of denial is that which comes from the friends of the abuser once the abuse has been exposed. This kind of denial is the first stage in the process of grief. The friends are wounded and betrayed, and they need to be treated with the greatest sensitivity because the chance they will become stuck in this stage increases the more they had invested in the relationship. The grieving process is a complex one because, deep in their hearts, they know they have lost a friend. However, they've also lost faith in their own ability to know what another person is truly like. They haven't just lost trust in other people, they've lost trust in themselves. To survive the emotional pain, the easiest thing to do is deny the victim's story. Sometimes it's helpful simply to say gently to these people, 'Please don't get stuck in grief.' That's often enough to bring them to a recognition of their own feelings and help them pass into the second stage of grief: anger. Usually they'll be angry at you, but so long as you realise this and don't react, it helps them to move on.

The third kind of denial is that expressed by the victim. It's a coping mechanism to avoid feeling overwhelmed by helplessness. Once a support system is in place, it's possible for this coping mechanism to suddenly disappear.

In the second and third cases, goodness, kindness and faithfulness from the victim's friends are critical. This is 'chesed', the Fruit of the Spirit that will provide the support for both the victim and the friends of the abuser to stop enabling and face the unpalatable truth.

Appendix 5
Belial and the number 153

In the Book of Enoch, the leader of the Watchers is called Samyaza. In the Dead Sea Scrolls from Qumran, he's called Belial. The Book of Genesis unfortunately sheds no light on the matter, simply calling the angels who descended to earth 'Benei Ha'Elōhīm', traditionally translated *sons of God*.

Until the sixteenth century when the decimal system became widespread throughout Europe, letters and numbers were not separate. Roman numerals were assigned certain values and, long before that, back in biblical times, both the Greek and Hebrew alphabets did double duty as both letters and numbers. Each letter had an assigned value. Consequently so did a word, a phrase or a sentence, and their values could be easily calculated by simply adding up the totals.

'Benei Ha'Elōhīm' adds up to 153, using the values of the letters in Hebrew gematria. In the understanding of ancient peoples, words with the same value were profoundly and deeply connected. As today we connect words through etymological trees, so back a few millennia ago, scholars connected words with the same mathematical totals.

Now 153 happens to be a very significant number both in ancient geometry and in the story of the resurrection. When Jesus cooked breakfast on the lakeshore for His disciples, He said:

> *'Bring some of the fish you've just caught.'... So Simon Peter went aboard and dragged the net to the shore. There were 153 large fish, and yet the net hadn't torn.*
>
> John 21:10–11 NLT

There's a great joke in this sentence—which unfortunately hasn't survived the centuries. At the time of Jesus, 153 was known as the 'measure of the fish'. The Greek inventor and geometer Archimedes had discovered that two intersecting circles that touched each other's centres formed a fish shape that always had a length-to-width ratio of $265/153$. Now this fun fact hides an elegant mathematical property. If we apply a trinity function to the skeleton of 153, a remarkable thing happens.

The skeleton of 153 is 1 and 5 and 3.

Under a trinity function (otherwise known as 'cubing') these become 1^3 and 5^3 and 3^3. Add these together:

$1^3 + 5^3 + 3^3 =$
$\qquad 1 \times 1 \times 1 + 5 \times 5 \times 5 + 3 \times 3 \times 3 =$
$\qquad\qquad 1 + 125 + 27 =$
$\qquad\qquad\qquad 153.$

Very few numbers come back to themselves—are 'resurrected'—from their skeletons under a trinity function, and 153 is the first of them. Jesus was using fish, of all things, to remind His disciples of the resurrection!

Now John, who wrote about this incident in his gospel, used a very special literary technique to frame up his writing. It was a Hebrew poetic device called *chiasmus* and it meant that his gospel is written in mirror scenes. There are matching bookends at the beginning and the end of his work.[73] Now it happens that the parallel to:

> *So Simon Peter went aboard and dragged the net to the shore. There were 153 large fish, and yet the net hadn't torn...*

is this section of the speech of John the Baptist:

> *'It is He who comes after me, the thong of whose sandal I am not worthy to untie.'*
>
> John 1:27 NASB

I have to admit that when I was first matching up the bookends, I dismissed these two lines as having nothing to do with one another. However, as it turned out they were the only unpaired thoughts in the entirety of the first and last chapter. It seemed unlikely that just one section had been missed, so I dug deeper.

What did untied sandals remind me of? They reminded me of bare feet and the Commander of the Army of the Lord saying to Joshua:

> *'Take off your sandals, for the place where you are standing is holy.'*
>
> Joshua 5:15 BSB

That, in turn, reminded me of God's promise:

> *'I have given you every place where the sole of your foot will tread, just as I promised to Moses.'*
>
> Joshua 1:3 BSB

Being of a suspicious turn of mind, which is possibly another way of attesting to some inspiration of the Holy Spirit, I added up the gematria and discovered that *'Every place where the sole of your foot will tread'* totals 1734 or 17x17x6. But if I include *'I have given'*, the total becomes 2600. Adding in 1 for the 'kollel',[74] the result is 2601 which is 17x153.

This suggests that a sandal—or sole—symbolises inheritance and, in confirmation of this, God's instruction to Moses is:

> *Joshua the son of Nun, who stands before you, he shall go in there. Encourage him, for he shall cause Israel to inherit it.*
>
> Deuteronomy 1:38 NKJV

Those last words *'he shall cause to inherit'* are one of a handful of Hebrew phrases totalling 153. Thus, through that match-up between loose sandals and 153 fish, John the apostle in his gospel echoed an ancient understanding of inheritance with reference to the new Joshua, Jesus of Nazareth.

The 'territory' Jesus had won back from Belial and the 'Benei Ha'Elōhīm' was not just the right and authority to govern the nations of the world with justice and peace, but included the privilege of resurrection and the inheritance of the Holy Spirit.

Belial wants that resurrection power and inheritance for his own family. So we must guard and keep it by constantly reaffirming our loyalty to God, just as Joshua did.

Endnotes

1. This is available for free download at gracedropswithanne.com

2. The Aramaic word for *a counsellor who uses divination or astrology* is 'adargazar' from ''iddar', *threshing floor*, and 'gzar', *determine, judge*. The combination, which derives from the Persian and may have military overtones, is *the one who determines or makes a judgment on the threshing floor*. The threshing floor was thus linked to astrology and divination.

3. This method of attack by an abuser is so predictable that the analyst Ben Nimmo conceptualised it as four 'D's: dismiss, distort, distract, dismay.

4. Bible translators tend to make abstractions of beings that are personified in Scripture: beings like Death and Time, Pestilence and War.

5. There is a difference between Kronos, the Titan and father of Zeus, and Chronos, the Greek godling of time, but they have been conflated for so many millennia that I believe we have to deal with them spiritually together. Whether we see them as one or two is therefore not particularly relevant.

6. James VanderKam, Enoch: *A Man For All Generations*, University of South Carolina Press 1995

7. Christa Brown, a longtime advocate who experienced sexual abuse by her pastor at 16, said her encounters with denominational leaders who shunned and disbelieved her 'left a legacy of hate' and communicated 'you are a creature void of any value—you don't matter.' As a result,

she said, instead of her faith providing solace, her faith has become 'neurologically networked with a nightmare.' She referred to it as 'soul murder'. (See: christianitytoday.com/news/2022/may — accessed 1 June 2022)

8. Like so many other words, it doesn't translate well across into other languages. Paul obviously had trouble when he was writing to the Galatians and realised there wasn't a corresponding Greek word that had the same overtones and nuances. There are English words that match the Greek ones but not for the Hebrew original. Myles Coverdale invented a word for Hebrew 'chesed' for the first complete printed English rendition of the Bible. His *lovingkindness* was then taken up by the King James translators.

9. Michael S Heiser, *Reversing Hermon: Enoch, the Watchers & the Forgotten Mission of Jesus Christ*, Defender Publishing 2017, commenting on Torleif Elgvin's overview of the data covering these centuries.

10. Sahjaza, Semihazah, Shemihazah, Shemyazaz, Shemyaza, Sêmîazâz, Semjâzâ, Samjâzâ and Semhazah. The name Shemyaza(z) means *the name has seen* or *he sees the name* or *my name is strength.*

11. William Horbury indicated that another name for Belial was Gog. See: Michael S Heiser, *Reversing Hermon: Enoch, the Watchers & the Forgotten Mission of Jesus Christ*, Defender Publishing 2017

12. It was considered canonical in Ethiopia where copies were preserved.

13. They are also mentioned in Psalm 106:37 as well as Deuteronomy 32:17, both times in relation to child or animal sacrifices. The word conveys a sense of *acting with violence* or *laying waste* but, beyond the Hebrew world, it was linked with morally ambivalent guardian spirits.

> 'Although the word is traditionally derived from the root šWD ... it was possibly a loan-word from Akkadian in which the word *shedu* referred to a protective, benevolent spirit. The word may also derive from the "Sedim, Assyrian guard spirits" as referenced according to lore, "Azazel slept with Naamah and spawned Assyrian guard spirits known as *sedim*." With the translation of Hebrew texts into Greek, under influence of Zoroastrian dualism, *shedim* were translated into *daimonia* with implicit negativity. Otherwise, later in Judeo-Islamic culture, *shedim* became the Hebrew word for Jinn with a morally ambivalent attitude.' Rosemary Ellen Guiley, *The Encyclopedia of Angels*, Facts on File Books, 2004

14. This is my own interpretation of the word.

15. Personally I think the confusion over the leadership of the Watchers—mostly said to be Samyaza, but occasionally cited as Azazel—probably arises because of this hint of *goat*. Azazel was the scapegoat and Samyaza was, in my view, associated with a *goat* through Belial. Since I have not found any source that translates Belial as *goat lord*, my explanation for my belief that this is what it evoked, if not what it meant, is as follows.

    > Belial is transliterated from Hebrew as 'beliyyaal', said to be from 'beli', *wear out*, and 'yaal', *confer* or *profit*. However, 'yaal', *confer*, is spelled precisely the same in the original Hebrew as 'yael', *mountain goat*. The first part, 'beli' is said to be from 'balah', *worn out*. However, Bel is the name of the chief deity of Babylon, and is a contraction of 'ba'al', *lord* or *owner*. Regardless of the etymology of Belial, I believe that it evoked *lord of goats* to any Hebrew listener.

16. Thomas R. Horn, commenting on David Flynn's suggestion, says: 'In other words, they wanted to incarnate themselves into the material world. The New Testament also suggests this idea when Jude, the brother of our Lord, wrote, "And the angels which kept not their

first estate, but left their own habitation [*oikētērion*]" (Jude 6). This Greek term, *oikētērion*, is used by Paul in 2 Corinthians 5:2 to denote the transfigured body given to believers in heaven. This implies that these fallen angels indeed sought to extend part of themselves into earthly bodies. The rendering 'fit extensions' seems applicable when the whole of the ancient record is understood to mean that the Watchers wanted to leave their proper sphere of existence.' skywatchtv.com/2021/05/16/deception9/#_edn1 (accessed 16 April 2022)

17. This thought is reflected in the writings and podcasts of Michael Heiser.

18. It's fascinating to read the various commentaries that say the Watchers who descended were corrupted by their cohabitation with women. Not that they came deliberately to corrupt the women and all mankind through them. This is, yet again, an interesting reversal of the victim-perpetrator dynamic.

19. The word 'Janissary' itself comes from the Turkish language and means *new troops*. The Janissaries were a part of Ottoman culture for over half a millennium. As a distinct body of troops, they haven't existed for about a century and a half but their influence still pervades the Muslim world. While the Janissaries existed, the Sultans never had to risk the lives of their own people in combat. They used the children of their enemies against them.

This mode of building an army went on for so long a thinking grew up that still exists: *our enemies will resource the war against themselves.* That deep expectation is the spiritual driving force behind the Gallipoli campaign where until just a few months beforehand, the British were training the Turks—in fact, supplying them with the very sea mines that took out so many naval vessels and made the land attack at Gallipoli a necessity. That expectation has also been spiritual fuel for the rise of the Taliban, the rise of ISIS, who were both armed and resourced by their enemies. In recent times, the staggering arsenal of weapons and military hardware left behind and intact by the Americans after their withdrawal from Afghanistan is not simply incompetence, it's this spirit at work. On another level, there's the constant media defence of Muslims, often through silence, while barraging and exposing Christians and Jews. And of course you'll probably recognise the work of this spirit in our schools, where parental rights have been so totally overturned in the relentless drive for 'equality'.

20. Three weeks after the September 11 attacks in 2001, a spate of letters arrived at various media outlets and senators' offices. They contained a deadly fine white powder, anthrax, which killed five people. The media frenzy fingered Saddam Hussein as the culprit, although the FBI investigation concluded the most likely source was a US military lab. It was known that Hussein had anthrax because fourteen years previously Secretary of Defense Donald Rumsfeld had given him an anthrax arsenal when Rumsfeld had been the CEO of a pharmaceutical company. (Robert F Kennedy Jr, *The Real Anthony Fauci: Bill Gates, Big Pharma, and the Global War on Democracy and Public Health*, Skyhorse Publishing 2021) Admittedly it is unlikely to have been bioterrorism by Saddam Hussein, but if it had been, then this is just one of many examples of the United States resourcing the war against itself.

21. Charles Eisenstein comments: 'The Roman historian Tacitus wrote, "It is a principle of nature to hate those whom you have injured." By the same token, it is a principle of nature to despise those one has deceived.'

    Fintan O'Toole further comments on leaders who treat the law with contempt: 'There is one rule… crucial to the maintenance of power. Never, ever, make the people who place their faith in you feel like fools… Or, to put it another way, never let the people who think they are making a sacrifice realise that in fact they *are* the sacrifice… there is no forgiveness for that terrible moment when you realise that the anguish you have endured for the greater good was, to those in authority, just a mark of your credulousness and inferiority.'

22. If the Divine Council is a new concept for you, allow me to recommend Michael Heiser's scholarly and academic book, *The Unseen Realm: Recovering the Supernatural Worldview of the Bible*, Lexham Press 2015.

23. See Abarim Publications, abarim-publications.com/Meaning/Sodom.html (accessed 21 September 2020). Other possible meanings include *flaming, burnt, furrows, wet fields, breasts* or *assembly*.

24. If you know any Hebrew, you will realise that 'shedim' starts with the letter *shin*, as does 'shittim'. Both 'Sodom' and 'Siddim' on the other hand start with the letter *samekh*. As is argued in my other books, God is not an etymologist but a poet (see Ephesians 2:10, which in Greek says, *'We are His poetry...'*). While the spelling and grammar of Hebrew are very important, the logic of word science should never become such an obsession that poetic devices such as rhymes and assonance are excluded and even despised. These forms are not only the basis of so much prophecy but are also natural to the stream-of-consciousness flow of human thought. So the fact that 'sodom' starts with a *samekh* and 'shedim' with a *shin* is, I believe, in this instance, immaterial. It could well be a dialect similar to *shibboleth* and *sibboleth*. (See: Judges 12:6)

25. The healing of Bartimaeus and that of Zacchaeus, both of which occurred in Jericho. Space constraints do not permit me to discuss the implications here. Those miracles will be addressed in an upcoming volume in the *Jesus and the Healing of History* series.

26. Exodus 32:36

27. Name covenant is explained in detail in the third book in this series, *Name Covenant: Invitation to Friendship—Strategies for the Threshold #3*. One of the important details it explains is that name covenant with God is never a solitary event; it is always accompanied by a threshold covenant six days later.

28. Luke 4:3 NASB

29. Genesis 1:25

30. Malachi 3:10

31. Isaiah 7:12

32. There is also 'zeman' for *appointed time*, but it mainly occurs in Esther and Nehemiah, indicating it is a later word.

33. The time Jesus spent in the desert therefore exactly corresponded to the anniversary of the forty-day period Moses spent on Mount Sinai while receiving the second set of stone tablets with the commandments engraved on them. This period, extending from 1 Elul to 10 Tishrei, is still observed today with fasting and prayer and is known as 'Teshuvah', *repentance* and *reconnection*. The Christian community developed a very close parallel to this Jewish practice at a different time of year: the forty-day period called 'Lent'.

34. Going by the Jewish cycle of years, not our modern reckoning that starts in January. The Hebrew calendar is a luni-solar one and so the dates correspond to our Gregorian calendar only once every nineteen years.

35. Name covenant is an ancient friendship ritual, common to many societies up until the nineteenth century. A remnant of it is the adoption by a woman of her husband's family name on marriage. It involves a name exchange and is explained in detail in the third book in this series, *Name Covenant: Invitation to Friendship—Strategies for the Threshold #3*.

36. See: douglashamp.com/at-satans-command-a-new-translation-of-the-mt-hermon-inscription (accessed 10 January 2022) The top of Mount Hermon is not currently accessible, since it is the border between Israel, Syria and Lebanon. A United Nations post is there. Nevertheless the description of what Jesus and His disciples did is deduced from the drawing of the Qasr Antar structure on the mountaintop made by Charles Warren. During an expedition in 1869, Warren found the temple, and realised that pilgrims in past times would have had to enter it before continuing upwards towards the peak. They were then forced into a peculiar anti-clockwise spiral pattern, in order to reach the summit. The southern peak's rocky terrain had been scooped out to receive ritual libations to the god or gods of the mount. In confirmation of this theory, Warren discovered within the area a strange *stele* (alternatively spelled *stela*; a stone pillar or marker), engraved on one side in ancient Greek. Douglas Hamp's translation suggests it refers to a bull-god, not just a generic deity or group of them.

37. See: Derek Gilbert, *The Second Coming of Saturn: The Great Conjunction, America's Temple, and the Return of the Watchers*, Defender Publishing, 2021

38. oneforisrael.org/holidays/yeshua-and-the-sukkot-water-drawing-festival (accessed 7 May 2022)

39. *Forerunner Commentary.* See: bibletools.org/index.cfm/fuseaction/topical.show/rtd/cgg/id/3831/wine-symbolism-of-.htm (accessed 1 May 2022)

40. Edward Lipiński, *El's Abode: Mythological Traditions related to Mount Hermon and to the Mountains of Armenia*, Orientalis Lovaniensa Periodica II, 1971

41. See: randomgroovybiblefacts.com/the_cloudy_tabernacle.html (accessed 29 April 2022) Springfield also points out that this suggests Jonah delivered his message to Nineveh at Yom Kippur, the Day of Atonement,

because of the 'sukkah' he builds afterwards. See: randomgroovybiblefacts.com/yonah_kippur.html

42. Actually, the Hebrew word, 'kaph', the particular term for *cornerstone* I'm referring to here, means a whole lot more than *covering*. It means *hollow of the hand*, or *palm; sole of the foot, palm branch, a shallow pan* or *bowl, a threshold* or *basin*. It's derived from a word for *curve*, and related to *atonement, pitch, frost, head covering, rafter* and *young lion*.

43. See: Dwight Pryor in the article, *Jesus—The Fullness of Tanakh*, in the book, *Roots and Branches: Explorations in the Jewish Context of the Christian Faith*. This article discusses the Transfiguration at some length, pointing out that the language used by God during that momentous event is that of a midwife. He further points out that, just a few days prior to this, Jesus had asked His disciples who people thought He was and also who they thought He was. Several answers are given—but God's answer to Jesus' question is not revealed until the Transfiguration. God's statement is a combination of phrases from the Law (Moses), the Prophets (Isaiah) and the sacred writings (Psalms). In addition, there are three witnesses to the Father's words, reflecting this same threefold division of Law, Prophets and sacred writings: Moses, Elijah and the Father Himself.

44. *'Your Word is settled in heaven.'* So says Psalm 119:89 NKJV. If God's word is not settled, if seasons can be changed or time altered, then the throne of God is up for grabs. This is why the anti-Christ powers are so keen to change times, seasons and weather—so that God can be charged with covenant violation. *'This is what the Lord says: "If you can break My covenant with the day and My covenant with the night, so that day and night no longer come at their appointed time, then My covenant with David My servant—and My covenant with the Levites who are priests ministering before me—can be broken and David will no longer have a descendant to reign on his throne."... "If I have*

> *not made My covenant with day and night and established the laws of heaven and earth, then I will reject the descendants of Jacob and David My servant and will not choose one of his sons to rule over the descendants of Abraham, Isaac and Jacob.'"* (Jeremiah 33:20–21; 26–27 NIV)

45. Chaim Bentorah, *A Hebrew Teacher Looks at Stargates, Time Travel, and Alternate Universes: Biblical Word Studies With Chaim Bentorah*, True Potential Books 2021

46. This water libation would help explain why it was a flood that destroyed the earth. The basic principle of law at the heart of creation is 'you reap what you sow'—not the greatest of metaphors when discussing water which can hardly be 'sown' but let's forge on with the idea regardless. This law has a lemma, 'You reap in the same kind as you sow' and is partnered by the multiplication principle, 'You reap more than you sow.'

In consideration of these three principles, worship on a mountaintop involving 'water descending' would bring in its wake the following consequence: water descending to mountaintops and rising above them.

47. Dionysius-Zagreus, the wild wine-loving deity who revelled in both orgy and destructive mutilation, was the oldest of the godlings of Crete. One of his names was *'The True Vine'*, a title Jesus later claimed back. He demonstrated at this time during Sukkot His right to it.

48. The anti-Christ spirit will try to change times and timing.

49. Again, going by Jewish years, not our modern reckoning starting in January. Sukkot was in the first month of the Jewish civic calendar (distinct from the sacred calendar), and occurs around September. The following Sukkot (or perhaps the one after) Jesus was up Mount Hermon, so an extra 12 months may need to be included here.

50. Aaron Demsky, *Geba, Gibeah, and Gibeon: An Historico-Geographic Riddle*, Bulletin of the American Schools of Oriental Research No. 212 (Dec., 1973) jstor.org/stable/1356308 (accessed 11 May 2021)

51. Deuteronomy 13: 16

52. Aaron Demsky, *Geba, Gibeah, and Gibeon: An Historico-Geographic Riddle*, Bulletin of the American Schools of Oriental Research No. 212 (Dec., 1973) jstor.org/stable/1356308 (accessed 11 May 2021)

53. If this is correct, then the English word, *goblet*, may derive from the same root. This is not unlikely, given that *cup* may come from 'kaph', the root word for *palm of the hand, sole of the foot* and *cornerstone* as well as *covering*. See: Isaac Mozeson, *The Word: The Dictionary that Reveals the Hebrew Source of English*, S.P.I. Books 2001

54. 1 Peter 2:17

55. In the Aramaic version of 1 Enoch, the angel who taught spell-binding (and also root-cutting) was Shemihazah (Samyaza), the leader of the Watchers. (See: Ida Fröhlich, *The Figures of the Watchers in the Enochic Tradition* (1-3 Enoch), academia.edu/3411829 — accessed 13 May 2022) In other texts, the leader is identified as Belial. In the time of Christ, the combination of spells and drugs (produced from the roots) was considered to be 'pharmakeia', the origin of our word *pharmaceutical* but which originally meant *sorcery*.

56. 2 Corinthians 6:17 NIV

57. Hagar may also mean *flight* or *the one dragged away*.

58. Of course, Jerusalem naturally had its own cornerstone, but it wasn't a cornerstone for the nation in its own right. It wasn't a 'first' city in any sense.

59. It's traditionally considered that the Salem ruled by Melchizedek was the same as Jerusalem, but that is not necessarily the case. It may be the city on the Jordan River,

where John the Baptist moved to after leaving Bethany-beyond-the-Jordan. Likewise, while it is assumed the Jerusalem of the Canaanite king Adoni-zedek is the same as David's Jerusalem, there is not enough information to be sure.

60. Hebron was where Absalom declared himself king, suggesting that it retained considerable status as David's first capital.

61. See Numbers 36:7

62. It would have been militarily unwise to hand the fortress over to the people of Benjamin who possibly still harboured a desire for the House of Saul to resume their former prominence. Giving power to a potentially untrustworthy tribe would have been a strategic mistake. But that doesn't make right the movement of David's capital from his clan's territory into someone else's. That says: *what's mine is mine and what's yours is mine*. In addition, it gave the people of Benjamin yet another reason to believe Judah was out to get them. The Benjaminites had been so traumatised by the genocide in the days of the Judges that they clearly came to trust outsiders, the people of Edom, far more than they did any of their brother tribes. Saul's chief herdsman, for example, was an Edomite while the names in his family line reflect the deities of Edom. (See: *Dealing with Resheph: Spirit of Trouble* in this series for more details.)

63. Isaiah 28:13 ESV

64. Nahum 1:11 and Nahum 1:15.

65. Like 'the yarid' being a better reading for 'Jared', it's quite possible 'the gilgal' is a better reading for Gilgal. It's not the name of a fixed place but a word to indicate the nearest stone 'circle' where festivities took place. 'Circle' may well be a misnomer and may perhaps simply indicate a stone memorial that could be walked around.

Archaeologist Adam Zertal suggested that the huge ancient *footprint* shapes found in the Jordan Valley were 'gilgals'—which he interpreted as sacred spaces where the tabernacle was pitched, a sacrificial altar was located and which were surrounded by a stone pathway where it was possible for people to walk around and around, singing and rejoicing, on festival days. (See: thetorah.com/article/gilgal-yhwhs-footprints-in-the-land-of-israel — accessed 12 November 2021)

66. These alternatives signal the strong possibility that the battle of Deborah and Barak against Sisera, the commander of the Canaanite king of Hazor, involved a divine annulment of a covenant with Death. Although the biblical description of the battle itself looks quite straightforward, merely commenting that the Lord 'routed' the armies by the sword, Deborah's song mentions the miraculous nature of the intervention, so reminiscent of both Joshua's battle against the five kings and the siege of Jerusalem by the Assyrians.

In addition, there is a hint in Deborah's song that this was a conflict with the giants:

> *From the heavens the stars fought,*
> *from their courses they fought against Sisera.*
> *The river Kishon swept them away,*
> *the age-old river, the river Kishon.*
> *March on, my soul; be strong!*
> *Then thundered the horses' hooves—*
> *galloping, galloping go his mighty steeds.*
> *'Curse Meroz,' said the angel of the Lord.*
> *'Curse its people bitterly,*
> *because they did not come to help the Lord,*
> *to help the Lord against the mighty.'*
>
> Judges 5:20–23 NIV

The last word, 'gibborim', may simply mean *a powerful man* but it is also the word that designated the 'heroes of old' in Genesis 6 who were the children of the *nephilim*, and thus angel-human hybrids. While the stopping or reversing of time is not mentioned in this song of Deborah's, earthquakes, torrents of water, stars fighting and cloud covering are—thus combining in one story three elements from three different battles fought at Beth Horon, as well as significant aspects of the angelic defeat of the Assyrian army during the reign of Hezekiah.

67. nature.com/articles/nm0900_971 (accessed 18 May 2022)

68. abortion.procon.org/source-biographies/mother-teresa (accessed 2 November 2019)

69. Dr Keith Ablow, *"Men Should Be Able to Veto Abortions,"* Foxnews.com, July 22, 2011. foxnews.com/opinion/2011/07/22/men-should-be-able-to-veto-abortions/#ixzz2IeIii0fe (accessed 22 November 2019)

70. afterabortion.org/most-studies-show-abortion-linked-to-increased-mental-health-problems/ (accessed 10 January 2020)

71. Michael Paget, Opinion, ABC News, 5 March, 2017

72. Frank Pavone, *Abolishing Abortion: How You Can Play a Part in Ending the Greatest Evil of Our Day*, Nelson Books 2015

73. I don't know of any scholarly work that mentions this as a totality. Some works mention individual parallels, but not that the entire gospel is devised as a Hebrew poem with chiastic mirrored elements around a central double peak involving two I AM statements. I decided to write a book on the phenomenon myself, in the naïve belief it'd be a very short work since it would be simple matter of matching up the same broad brushstrokes of themes and names. However, I soon realised it's a massive undertaking because the matching is so fine-tuned and detailed. The alignments were much closer than I'd expected. I can't say for sure this is the case all the way through the gospel, but I can say that the first chapter and the last chapter and a

half are exquisitely lined up. I hope eventually to be able to publish the work I've done so far, but it is so dense and academic—when I wanted to make it quite devotional in nature—that I'm hoping to see a way of making it simpler.

74. The addition of 1 for a *kollel* is not simply for the word itself but for the silence within the word. (See: David Patterson, *Wrestling with the Angel: Towards a Jewish Understanding of the Nazi Assault on the Name*, Paragon House 2006)

If you found this book helpful, other books in this series may prove useful too as you address the issues that bar your way into your calling:

Dealing with Python:
Spirit of Constriction

Strategies for the Threshold #1

On the threshold into your unique calling in life a dark spiritual sentinel waits. Scripture names it 'Python'—it has a God-given right to be there and test your significant choices. Trying to cast it out of a situation is useless.

Paul encountered it just as the Gospel was transitioning across a major threshold: the watershed moment when Christianity moved from Asia to Europe.

This long-awaited book explores the tactics of Python, as well as its agenda. It offers insight into what this spirit hopes to get from you and how you can rectify past mistakes involving this constricting, cunning enemy.

Dealing with Ziz:
Spirit of Forgetting

Strategies for the Threshold #2

The most significant threshold point of life is the doorway into God's unique calling for us. He invites us through covenant to fulfil the destiny we were born to achieve.

However, many of us fall at the threshold, rather than pass over it. We experience constriction, wasting, retaliation and forgetting—to such a degree it's easy to doubt the promises of God.

Dealing with Ziz examines the spiritual implications of forgetting in relation to threshold covenants. Since the opposite of remembering is dismembering—dismembering of truth—the spirit of forgetting is able to block access to our calling.

Yet there is an answer, a Fruit of the Spirit that overcomes Ziz.

Name Covenant:
Invitation to Friendship

Strategies for the Threshold #3

Abram became Abraham. Jacob became Israel. Simon beame Peter.

Name covenanting seems at first like an archaic, long-discarded practice that disappeared in the first century around the time Saul became Paul. The patriarchs and apostles exchanged names and so received new destinies. But that was then. And this is now.

However name covenanting never went away.

Robert Louis Stevenson became Terjitera. Paul Gauguin became Tioka. James Cook became Terreeoboo. Arthur Phillip became Woollaraarre.

These recent examples throw light on this ancient practice of friendship and kinship. They show us that, when God offers a new name, more than simply a new calling is attached. It's an invitation to friendship with Him.

If you're wondering how to overcome the issues of the threshold and the associated ungodly covenants, this book has the answer. Other books help you recognise the problem, this one points out the first step on the path.

Hidden in the Cleft:
True and False Refuge

Strategies for the Threshold #4

Jesus had a refuge—a safe haven—He retreated to when His life was in danger.

What does His choice reveal about where best to find sanctuary in times of trouble? What is the significance of the hiding place He used for an entire season? How can we discern the difference between a true and false refuge?

Removal of our false refuges is the first step towards achieving our life's calling—the divine purpose for which God created us. Yet all too often we fail to recognise how we've defaulted to a false refuge when disappointment strikes.

This book offers practical help, hope and encouragement towards achieving your destiny in Christ.

Dealing with Leviathan:
Spirit of Retaliation

Strategies for the Threshold #5

Retaliation, reprisal, retribution—many of us express the ferocity of our encounters with the spirit of Leviathan with such words. Most believers are stunned by savagery of the backlash they experience, and are baffled by God's seeming failure to intervene.

Reparation, recompense, restitution, restoration—these promised corrections to injustice are smashed just as they seem within reach. Why does this happen?

As we examine Scripture, we find that Leviathan is an officer of God's royal court. When we violate the consecration of that Holy Place, it has the legal right to remove us. It does not do so gently.

Dealing with Leviathan offers insight into overcoming this spirit of the deep.

Dealing with Resheph:
Spirit of Trouble

Strategies for the Threshold #6

Resheph is mentioned seven times in Scripture. A fallen seraph and throne guardian, it is identified here as a hidden face of Leviathan, the spirit that counterattacks against dishonour. Symbolised as a stag and an archer, Resheph is connected with flames and fire, fever, financial distress, mental illness, drought and scorching heat as well as the underworld.

Jesus warred against this spirit at least seven times. It's easy to miss these battles because it's easy to miss the prophecies Jesus was fulfilling and the mention of Resheph associated with them.

This is a companion volume to *Dealing With Leviathan* and examines the obstacles we face on the threshold into our calling.

Dealing with Azazel:
Spirit of Rejection

Strategies for the Threshold #7

'I am your only friend.'

That's the playbook line that works so superbly for the spirit of rejection. Most of us fall for it without ever realising our coping mechanisms—fight, flight, freeze, flatter, forestall or forget—are actually undermining our every effort to overcome this entity. So how can we subdue the spirit of rejection in our lives without sabotaging ourselves in the process?

This seventh book in the series, *Strategies for the Threshold*, is the most highly anticipated volume so far. It addresses the nature of the spirit, its wider agenda, its spiritual legal rights, and its propensity for following after us to undo the good that we do.

www.ingramcontent.com/pod-product-compliance
Lightning Source LLC
Chambersburg PA
CBHW021141080526
44588CB00008B/167